Communications
in Computer and Information Science   389

Commenced Publication in 2007
Founding and Former Series Editors:
Alfredo Cuzzocrea, Dominik Ślęzak, and Xiaokang Yang

More information about this series at http://www.springer.com/series/7899

María José Abásolo · Raoni Kulesza (Eds.)

Applications and Usability of Interactive TV

Third Iberoamerican Conference, jAUTI 2014
and Third Workshop on Interactive Digital TV
Held as Part of Webmedia 2014
João Pessoa, PB, Brazil, November 18–21, 2014
Revised Selected Papers

 Springer

Editors
María José Abásolo
National University of La Plata
La Plata
Argentina

Raoni Kulesza
Federal University of Paraíba
João Pessoa, Paraíba
Brazil

ISSN 1865-0929   ISSN 1865-0937 (electronic)
Communications in Computer and Information Science
ISBN 978-3-319-22655-2   ISBN 978-3-319-22656-9 (eBook)
DOI 10.1007/978-3-319-22656-9

Library of Congress Control Number: 2015951761

Springer Cham Heidelberg New York Dordrecht London

Printed on acid-free paper

Springer International Publishing AG Switzerland is part of Springer Science+Business Media
(www.springer.com)

Preface

The Third Iberoamerican Conference on Applications and Usability of Interactive TV (jAUTI 2014) and the Third Workshop on Interactive Digital TV (WTVDI) were part of Webmedia 2014, the 20th Brazilian Symposium on Multimedia and the Web, which was held during November 18–21, 2014 in João Pessoa (Paraíba, Brazil).

WTVDI had its first edition during the 18th SIBGRAPI in 2005 and its second edition in 2010 during the 16th Webmedia. This last event provided support to jAUTI 2014, the third edition of a scientific event organized by the RedAUTI Thematic Network on Applications and Usability of Interactive Digital Television that is sponsored by the CYTED Ibero American Program of Science and Technology for Development.

RedAUTI currently consists of 238 researchers from 39 groups — 32 universities and seven companies — from Spain, Portugal, and ten Latin American countries. These proceedings contain a collection of extended selected papers originally presented at jAUTI 2014 that cover the development and deployment of technologies related to interactive digital TV. The selection rate was 38 % and the extended selected papers were peer reviewed to assure the high quality of this publication.

June 2015   María José Abásolo
                                                                          Raoni Kulesza

Organization

Program Chairs

María José Abásolo   National University of La Plata, Argentina
Raoni Kulesza   Federal University of Paraíba, Brazil

Program Committee

Jorge Abreu   University of Aveiro, Portugal
Pedro Almeida   University of Aveiro, Portugal
José Luis Arciniegas   University of Cauca, Colombia
Mónica Aresta   University of Aveiro, Portugal
Sandra Baldassarri   University of Zaragoza, Spain
Ivan Bernal   National Polytechnic School, Ecuador
Sebastian Betti   Sinapsis UX Research Team, Argentina
Sandra Casas   National University of Southern Patagonia, Argentina
Cesar Collazos   University of Cauca, Colombia
Carlos Ferraz   Federal University of Pernambuco, Brazil
Guido Lemos   Federal University of Paraíba, Brazil
Francisco Montero   University of Castilla La Mancha, Spain
Rita Oliveira   University of Aveiro, Portugal
Gonzalo Olmedo   Army Polytechnic School, Ecuador
Douglas Paredes Marquina   University of Los Andes, Venezuela
Lorena Paz   National Technological University, Argentina
Francisco Jose Perales   University of the Balearic Islands, Spain
Miguel Angel Rodrigo   Alonso University of Córdoba, Spain
Pablo Rodriguez   University of the Republic, Uruguay
Cecilia Sanz   National University of La Plata, Argentina
Telmo Silva   University of Aveiro, Portugal
Alejandra Zangara   National University of La Plata, Argentina

Contents

IDTV Overview

Interactive TV Interoperability and Coexistence: The GLOBAL ITV Project

Alan César Belo Angeluci$^{(\boxtimes)}$, Gustavo Moreira Calixto,
Maria Luiza Morandini, Roseli de Deus Lopes, and Marcelo Knorich Zuffo

Escola Politécnica da Universidade de São Paulo, São Paulo, Brazil
aangeluci@usp.br, {calixto,luizam,roseli,mkzuffo}@lsi.usp.br

Abstract. One of the main challenges in the future of broadcast television is to encompass new technological platforms, standards and trends
in the multimedia content consumption landscape along with new user's
behaviors and habits. Second screen and multiplatform experiences,
social media and broadband contents arose as a permanent change and
must to be considered in the future business model. Nevertheless, interoperability and coexistence issues are critical and fundamental aspects that
must to be further implemented in a worldwide perspective, as many of
the television standards were developed to cover regional markets mainly,
creating restrictions to the content and applications sharing and barriers
to the technological compatible layers. The aim of this paper is to discuss
the ongoing work of "GLOBAL ITV: Interoperability of Interactive and
Hybrid TV systems - A new advanced scheme for future services and
applications in a global environment", an international research project
from Brazil and European Union countries that seeks to establish a new
ground in the interactive television model and platforms aiming a global
impact. The description is mainly focused on the work being carried out
in the interactive TV landscape definition, playout and set-top-box development, and shows how solutions developed differ from other established
models.

Keywords: Interoperability · Coexistence · Interactive television ·
GLOBAL ITV project

1 Introduction

Parallel to the switchover from analog to digital television, various interactive
digital television systems have been developed worldwide - some only recently,
some already more than a decade ago. The driving idea was to offer consumers
additional new features and multimedia services in the landscape of this popular
and widespread media [1].

As a result of the recent broadcast-broadband convergence trend, most TV
sets sold today are so-called Smart TVs or Connected TVs, supporting the current perspective of Internet integration into modern television sets and set-top

© Springer International Publishing Switzerland 2015
M.J. Abásolo and R. Kulesza (Eds.): jAUTI 2014, CCIS 389, pp. 3–16, 2015.
DOI: 10.1007/978-3-319-22656-9_1

boxes [2] [3]. However, every digital television and Smart TV systems has been deployed on their own technologies, needs and specific country laws.

Applications developed for one system are generally not compatible with another one. The impact of this limitation reflects in the lack of interoperability among services, such as between open-to-air TV, connected TV and various digital TV systems deployed worldwide.

A recent international research initiative, known as "GLOBAL ITV project", has the aim of establishing the ground of a feasible interoperable and coexisting platform in which different TV standards can perform their best technical resources and content together. This paper aims to present the main ideas and challenges of GLOBAL ITV project, work in progress and future approaches.

2   The GLOBAL ITV Project: Structure and Objectives

Brazilians and European Union groups of experts from academia and market companies, organizations and research institutes got together in the project conceptualization process, led by the Interdisciplinary Center in Interactive Technologies from the University of São Paulo (CITI-USP), Brazil, and the Institut für Rundfunktechnik (IRT), Germany[1].

The official project's name is "GLOBAL ITV: Interoperability of Interactive and Hybrid TV systems - A new advanced scheme for future services and applications in a global environment". Its management structure consists on dividing the activities under Working Packages (WPs), in order to provide rapid decision making on both operational and technical issues while maintaining essential mechanisms for consensus management on project strategy and on other decisions pertaining to the consortium as a whole. Each partner has different tasks and activities in the entire project, performing leadership or collaboration roles depending on the WP (Fig. 1).

The project comprises the understanding of the current and future iTV scenarios and the development, testing and evaluation of interoperable iTV applications. One of the project focuses is to observe how social media and second screen impacts the ITV content consumption, and how it can be improved considering content synchronization in multiple screens, for example. Throughout the project dissemination activities will be foreseen, including promoting the results of each phase of the investigation. Moreover, the GLOBAL ITV goal is to continuously delineate roadmaps on the exploitation of the results in several domains: business, new research opportunities, standardization at national and international landscapes and policy.

---

[1] Others Brazilians and European Union institutions are part of the project. On the Brazilian side, UNESP, UNICAMP, UFABC, UFPA, UCB are universities from the North, Central West and Southeast regions of Brazil. HXD is a content producer and LSI-TEC is scientific and technological institute. BAND TV a broadcasting company. From European side, FRAUNHOFER FOKUS (Germany), TARA Systems (Germany), W3C (France), EBU (Switzerland), TDF (France), A-CING (Spain), RETEVISION (Spain), Symelar (Spain).

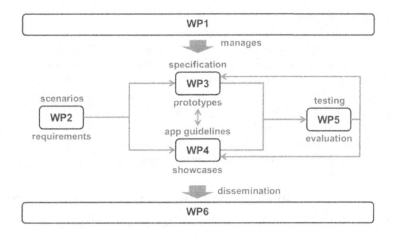

Fig. 1. GLOBAL ITV working package structure

3   Related Works

Scenario-based design method is usually a fruitful framework in order to conceptualize and develop systems [4]. In the case of ITV research, most of them are more technology-driven, focusing on technical constraints and solutions. Human factors have a strong impact in this issue as an ITV platform must to deal with user's behavior and consumption of new and interactive technologies.

ITV projects initiatives usually aim to "enhance already established systems regarding efficiency and performance mainly; they also look as goal to harmonize broadcasting systems, defining frameworks for seamless integration of broadcast with other networks and content, usually the Internet ones" [5]. Some initiative can be listed as example of these ITV projects being carried out around the world.

The Future of Broadcast Television Initiative (FOBTV) is an initiative led by Asian, American and European partners from different sectors, focusing on the development and prospection of a harmonized world standard, immersive experience and new services, smart interaction and personalization, and more efficient and flexible use of spectrum [6].

The Hybrid Broadcast Broadband Next Generation (HbbTV-Next) is an European initiative aims to lay the foundation of advanced services in hybrid and seamless integration of broadcast and Internet world [7]. HbbTV-Next research perspective is more user-driven and focused on the design process, exploring user-centred technologies for enriching the TV-viewing experience.

The ATSC 3.0 initiative is led by Advances Television Systems Committee which impacts countries and territories using the ATSC system, mainly in the North America. ATSC is more focused on standard implementation and technical feedback, aiming to provide more services for users through the increasing of band efficiency and compression performance [8].

4   Current Work

Although work is still under development, it is possible to highlight some traits already achieved for scientific contributions. In this section, three topics of interest in the project are deeper discussed. The first is the characterization of an interactive TV landscape both in Brazilian and European Union scenarios, which definition had an important impact in the selection of technologies and infrastructure to be used. The second and third ones are related to the interoperability and coexistence issues in the project: the solution developed for playout and the implementation that has been done for set-top-box.

4.1   The Consumer Broadcast and Broadband Landscape Worldwide

Television market is changing at slow pace but it is possible to assume that in the next comming years new technologies and political policies will have a strong influence in the development and direction of this market. Considering the technological aspect, international fairs such as NAB Show has shown the clear trend on TV sets with Ultra HD resolution (4K and 8K), pushing broadcasters to produce contents in high definition and meeting the demand for content in various platforms. Also, interactivity is still in the agenda but with hybrid TV or second-screen apps approach.

Understanding the Brazilian and European telecommunications scenario is imperative in order to establish the main challenges and opportunities for the GLOBAL ITV project. Some general matters such as TV digitalization, broadband networks expansion and smartphone acquisition growth are common features for both Europe and Brazil, though the cultural and legacy differences among those regions create different challenges.

In Brazil, when it comes to TV sets, 97.2% of households have a TV set, which are about 61 million homes. There is, though, a considerable difference in the distribution of such TV sets among the country extension. In the Southeast Region of Brazil, approximately 27,000 TV sets, while in the North Region, 93.3% of the households have a TV set, corresponding to 4,275 TV sets [9].

Although the TV equipment is present in almost every Brazilian home, the acquisition of digital TVs and set-top boxes should increase after the analog switch off, which is scheduled to happen between 2015 and 2018.

In European countries, TV sets are present in about 98% of households, being Greece and Cyprus the countries with the highest proportion, both with 100% of households with TVs, and Portugal, with 95%, and Finland, with 92% , the countries with lowest presence of TVs in homes [10].

According to the European Audiovisual Observatory, out of the 27 members of EU, 22 have already completed the analog switch off [11], but there are still significant differences between Eastern and Western Europe in the amount of households with digital TV reception. In Western Europe, about 89% of the households have digital TV, while in Eastern Europe it exists only in 44.5% of homes. The difference is even more pronounced when the terrestrial transmission is take in consideration: while it is present in 93% of all homes in Western

Europe, it appears only in 24% of Eastern European homes [12]. There is also the question that Europe is still overcoming the economic crisis, so growth is expected to happen in a mid-term period.

Regarding the broadband system in the Brazilian perspective, the fiber optics network was expanded stimulated by major games venues and the investment in the network is expected to be boosted as well. In Brazil, there is also the National Broadband Plan (PNBL) that intends to massify broadband connection throughout the country. The plan includes the increase of computers connected to the world wide web, expansion of fiber optics network and creation of low cost and lower speeds broadband connection [13].

On the European side, EUR 200 billion are expected to be spent in the improvement of broadband access. Depending on the population density of each area, the investment will come either from a private company, in the case the area has a large population density. These areas are called black areas. The gray and white areas follow the same analogy as the black areas and are, respectively, regions with mid population density and low population density. For the white areas, the structural funds are going to be employed to expand the network. As for the gray area, CEF will intervene as to mitigate the risk of such investments [14].

As for the current situation, Europe has a higher penetration of high speed broadband - 26.7% of households have high speed connections - than Brazil, which only has about 10% of homes with high speed broadband connection, although there is a significant difference between the extremes in European connection: Denmark and Netherlands with 40% of homes with high speed internet access versus Romania and Bulgaria with only 15%. Countries from Eastern Europe, though, have joined the EU not long ago, which means that a certain heterogeneity is to be expected in infrastructure [15].

The number of smart TVs in Europe has increased in the past few years in Western Europe, roughly 40% of all TVs sold from January, 2013 to April, 2013 were smart TVs and the this number tends to become even higher. Nowadays, the share of smart TVs in Europe is 59%, from which 92% run the HbbTV standard. HbbTV as an open standard has similar and comparable solutions if compared with proprietary systems such as GoogleTV/AppleTV [16].

According to projections of the STAI Institute [17] on a short-term plan (2015-2016), the hybrid system is expected to occupy 40% of the European television market, requiring the development of standardization of a hybrid TV receiver. In the Brazilian scenario, it is applicable to long-term (2020) in a particular niche market, as in the Brazilian market there is notable consolidation and growth of pay-TV, with 16 million consumers [18], and hybrids TV standards are in the initial process of presenting the system with broadcasters and broadband operators.

It is projected in the short-term that both Brazil and EU will consolidate the HTML5 as standard for developing interactive content in multiple system. The success of integration between television and the web depends on the ability to integrate the requirements of TV within the web standards [17].

Brazilian and European consumer markets are creating the required infrastructure in order to include hybrid TV systems. Europe is advanced in the analog shut-off, Brazil is schedule to perform the shutoff between 2015 and 2018. Both regions have plans to increase the broadband speed and penetration.

Analyzing the expected landscape of interactive TV in the period of 2016-2020 and possible use cases in different scenarios, it is possible to assume TV content will arrive to the users more and more through on-demand request although linear TV will continue being a consolidated way to reach the viewers, specially the upper-middle aged, the elderly and the people living in less developed areas. Also, the kind of TV programs will be very similar in all the parts of the world; in fact, there is a growing trend to devise a TV program thinking in the global scenario.

New portable devices, like smartphones and tablets, will allow to access to general or specific TV content on the move, but also at home acting as a personalized complement to the group TV watching experience.

The quick growth of quality broadband networks, the high efficiency of IP transmission, the more and more affordable prices and the protection of author rights, will make the streaming a preponderant way to reach to TV content in the Internet. It is worthy pointing that some areas in the globe will be still less connected and lacking better infrastructure. The interactive TV experience has grown a lot in the last years, but not due to the digital TV interactive systems (Open TV, Mediahighway, and more recently Global Executable MHP, Ginga or HBB-TV) but to the quick expansion of portable devices (smartphones and tablets) and to the three following uses:

- request of catch-up TV content.
- use of social networks, specially Twitter.
- use of second screens as a way to interact with the TV content (in analogue or digital reception)

4.2 Interoperability and Coexistence within the GLOBAL ITV Project

As described in the last sections, each interactive TV standards nowadays has been designed to cover specific regions and most of them are not ready to be compatible overseas. The GLOBAL ITV project has two main overall aspects regarding the achievements for a joint interactive TV platform: interoperability and coexistence. Interoperability means the possibility to perform different kind of applications in only one receiver. Coexistence is the feature that allows interactive TV applications from different standards to be run in the same platform - for instance, a scenario in which Ginga applications can call an HbbTV application to be run and vice-versa.

A first achievement to be reached is the interoperability. Fig. 2 illustrates a block diagram that represents a first step for a receiver where Ginga-NCL and HbbTV 1.x players are available. Ginga-NCL is a player for NCL/Lua based applications in the ISDB-Tb [19]. HbbTV contains a CE-HTML browser that

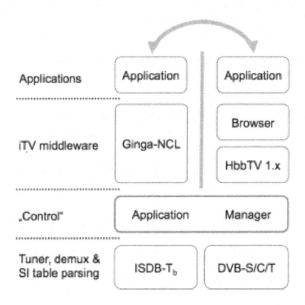

Fig. 2. Architecture stack diagram for Ginga-NCL and HbbTV interoperability and coexistence.

supports web-based interactive TV applications [20]. An Application Manager stack manages the processes to find applications signaling sent by broadcasters and also decides how this application can be download into the receiver: by Internet services or also by DSM-CC object carousel. In additional, the Application Manager should decide what is the right application player to be used. A recent study carried out by GLOBAL ITV project concluded that Ginga and HbbTV are similar in terms of application signaling and transport. Technically, a Ginga application can be transmitted in a DVB system and an HbbTV application can be transmitted in an ISDB-Tb system. Using the same architecture stack, the second achievement is to provide the coexistence aspect: a feature that an HbbTV application calls a Ginga-NCL application and vice-versa [21].

A third and final step is an architecture stack that enables to aggregate interactive TV application players through a web plug-in concept and also support web-based HTML5 application in a global environment, illustrated by Fig. 3. Moreover, HbbTV 1.x will be upgraded to HbbTV 2.0 offering more compatibility to web-based applications (mainly HTML5-based) and scenarios involving multiple screens [22] [23]. Not limited for Ginga-NCL and HbbTV, this architecture can support other interactive TV applications. Basically, ITV player plugins have interface to an HTML5-based browser, which can perform the necessary application rendering for receivers. Moreover, the idea of HTML5 applications in a global environment is supported by W3C (project partner) to be standardized worldwide as one of the expected outcomes of GLOBAL ITV project.

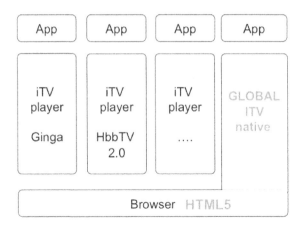

Fig. 3. Architecture stack with GLOBAL ITV project web plug-ins based final outcome

4.3 Playout

Both ISDB-Tb and DVB-T transmission are based on MPEG-2 transport stream. This transport stream is quite flexible on the transmission of metadata and different data formats that goes beyond audio and video only. This way, it is no surprise HbbTV and Ginga-NCL applications share a certain degree of similarity on their playout.

Ginga-NCL and HbbTV can both be downloaded via DSM-CC transmission, although HbbTV usually sends only the application link via broadcast and the rest of it is acquired by the TV or STB via broadband connection, while Ginga, on the other hand, loads the whole application on the data carousel and send it.

In the project, the playout tests main objective are to verify whether or not a HbbTV application will interfere with a Ginga-NCL application design environment. In other words, it means to check what sort of changes have to be done in the Ginga-NCL transport stream creation workflow so to include a HbbTV application. In order to do so, the testing was divided in two steps: lab tests and field tests. During the lab tests, an audio and video TS files are multiplexed with the application file, along with some signaling table and metadata, using opencaster, an open source stream manipulation tool library. The resulting TS is then modulated with an external board and then sent to the TV. As for the field tests, the signal will be broadcast in real time by a broadcaster, hence the application TS has to be outputted from the computer at demanded bit rate, so it can be multiplexed externally with the audio and video signal and then broadcasted.

4.4 Set-Top-Box and GLOBAL ITV Demonstrator

To attend the proposed architecture supporting Ginga-NCL and HbbTV interactive TV application players, a set-top-box (STB) is under development. In a first phase (illustrated in Fig. 2), the goal is to allow both HbbTV and Ginga-NCL software stacks to be executed in the STB, looking to achieve the interoperability and coexistence GLOBAL ITV aspects. Moreover, modules for tuner, transport stream demultiplexing and system information table parsing are provided by a GLOBAL ITV partner (TARA). Thus, in a first development stack, GLOBAL ITV aims to make available a receiver that allows to run Ginga-NCL and HbbTV applications and also allows to call each other for hybrid contexts. Two STB hardware arrangements are available: one with a ISDB-T receiver, for the Brazilian environment, and a DVB-T for the European environment. Fig. 5 presents the STB proof-of-concept.

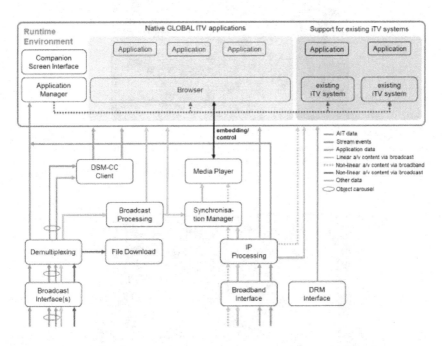

Fig. 4. GLOBAL ITV demonstrator architecture, from [5].

The illustration of Fig. 4 presents the GLOBAL ITV demonstrator architecture. Basically, the demonstrator has two main block: software stack for TV controlling and iTV application players. TV controlling software stack perform basic digital TV operations as well receive iTV application signaling through broadcast (ISDB-Tb or DVB) or broadband (Internet facilities). Thereafter, there are modules to handle application via Internet or DSM-CC as well as parse SI tables (metadata transmitted by broadcaster, for example the AIT table for application information). When an application is available to be run the Media player module calls the appropriated player based on AIT information (for instance Ginga-NCL, HbbTV, web-based players, etc.). Regarding the SI tables configuration for DSM-CC, the demonstrator are able to receive applications and parse

DSM-CC elementary streams from ISDB-Tb and DVB. Moreover, scenarios in which the broadcaster can send more than one application are expected and the demonstrator is able to allow interoperability (for instance, a Ginga-NCL application call HbbTV application and vice-versa). A detailed study about this issue, developed by GLOBAL ITV project, are presented in [21] and [5].

Fig. 5. GLOBAL ITV Demonstrator connected to a TV. The rendered cube represents graphical features that will be used by application players.

Fig. 6. GLOBAL ITV Demonstrator running Ginga-NCL application over a UNESP TV broadcast streaming

Considering the status of first phase development, the goal to run HbbTV and Ginga-NCL applications in a same set-top-box has been achieved. Fig. 6 shows a Ginga-NCL application running in the GLOBAL ITV demonstrator with a UNESP TV show, transmitted via ISBD-Tb. Regarding the HbbTV player, it is available on STB through an Opera web browser adapted to TV-centric applications purposes. Fig. 7 illustrates a HbbTV application running on GLOBAL ITV demonstrator. So the next step will be allow Ginga-NCL applications to invoke in runtime HbbTV applications and vice-versa where the broadcaster can set up both Ginga-NCL and HbbTV applications available for end users. In additional, the broadcaster should configure in SI tables which application is mandatory to be executed.

Fig. 7. GLOBAL ITV Demonstrator running HbbTV application over a North Brazil broadcaster streaming

Not limited to stress the GLOBAL ITV Demonstrator application players capability, media players tests has been carried out. Fig. 8 illustrates a high definition media stream playing in the GLOBAL ITV Demonstrator and Fig. 9 shows a video played in a Ginga-NCL application. Considering media playing capability available, the set-top-box also can perform as a media center focused for video on demand appliances.

In a second phase (illustrated in Fig. 3), the challenge is to advance application players to a web plug-in approach. The main idea is to use a HTML5 browser as a profile and support (e.g., Ginga-NCL and HbbTV through plug-ins). Using this approach, it is expected to reduce the time and effort for application players porting and accepting HTML5-native applications. This is an outcome foreseen to be achieved in the conclusion of GLOBAL ITV project works. A study is under development to allow Ginga-NCL applications able to be launched from a web-based player through plug-ins [24].

Not limited to implement and set up the demonstrator, conformance and end user tests are also under development, to validate platform compliance and users feedback.

Fig. 8. GLOBAL ITV Demonstrator playing a media stream.

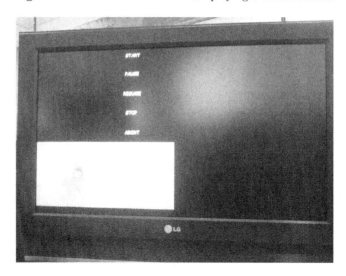

Fig. 9. GLOBAL ITV Demonstrator playing a media stream inside a Ginga-NCL application.

5 Final Remarks

Solutions described show how effectively the project approach differs from and improves on those initiatives discussed in the related works. GLOBAL ITV play-outs and STB are capable to support different and isolated interactive TV models, encompassing distinct signaling and applications into a common framework. This approach can generates long-term benefits for the whole chain of TV broadcasting market and interactive TV systems worldwide - content producers, manufacturers and final users. In a first step, an expected outcome is to develop an access terminal where is possible to run Ginga-NCL and HbbTV applications in both Brazilian and European digital TV system. Thereafter, in a final step, an receiver architecture that supports different interactive TV application players towards a web plug-in concept. Lately, GLOBAL ITV project has some preliminary outcomes publicly available regarding the prospection of usage scenarios [5]. A proof-of-concept, including a playout, receiver and sample applications is currently under development and will be released for demonstrations in 2015.

Acknowledgments. The authors would like to thanks to GLOBAL ITV project from the European Union's Seventh Framework Programme (FP7/2007-2013, call FP7-ICT-2013-10.2) under grant agreement number 614087 and from *Conselho Nacional de Desenvolvimento Científico e Tecnológico* (CNPq) under grant call MCTI/CNPq number 13/2012, project number 490088/2013-9.

References

1. Calixto, G.M., Angeluci, A.C., Costa, L.C., de Deus Lopes, R., Zuffo, M.K.: Cloud computing applied to the development of global hybrid services and applications for interactive TV. In: 2013 IEEE 17th International Symposium on Consumer Electronics (ISCE), pp. 283–284. IEEE (2013)
2. de Carvalho, E.R., et al.: The brazilian digital television system access device architecture. Journal of the Brazilian Computer Society **12**(4), 95–113 (2007)
3. Costa, L.C., Maruffa, A., Carvalho, W., Zuffo, M.K.: A framework design for connected television. In: 2012 IEEE International Conference on Consumer Electronics (ICCE), pp. 590–591. IEEE (2012)
4. Sears, A., Jacko, J.A.: The human-computer interaction handbook: fundamentals, evolving technologies and emerging applications. CRC Press (2007)
5. High-level description of the GLOBAL ITV landscape. D2.1 report, September 2014. http://www.globalitv.org/deliverables/publications/
6. Zhang, W., Wu, Y., Hur, N., Ikeda, T., Xia, P.: FOBTV: Worldwide efforts in developing next-generation broadcasting system (2014)
7. van Deventer, M., de Wit, J., Guelbahar, M., Cheng, B., Marmol, F.G., Köbel, C., Köhnen, C., Rozinaj, G., Stockleben, B.: Towards next generation hybrid broadcast broadband, results from FP7 and HBBTV 2.0. In: IBC 2013 Conference, Amsterdam, Netherlands (2013)
8. Bae, J., You, W., Kwon, O.H.: Research on the functional design of the next generation terrestrial mobile hd television. In: 2012 International Conference on ICT Convergence (ICTC), pp. 280–283. IEEE (2012)
9. de Geografia e Estatstica IBGE, I.B.: Pesquisa nacional por amostra de domiclios (2012)
10. Commission, E.: Digital agenda for europe (2012). http://ec.europa.eu/digital-agenda/digital-agenda-europe
11. Commission, E.: 2012 yearbook (2013). http://www.digitaltvnews.net/?p=22383
12. DieMedienanstalten: Digitisation: broadcasting and the internet - thesis, antithesis, synthesis (2013)
13. Programa nacional de banda larga (pnbl) - inicio, March 2012. http://www.mc.gov.br/programa-nacional-de-banda-larga-pnbl

14. Comission, E.: Connecting europe facility: investing in europeans growth (2014–2020) (2012)
15. Barometro cisco de banda larga 2.0. cisco June 2013. http://goo.gl/J2tgfP
16. TV-Plattform, D.: Marktanalyse smart-tv: Eine bestandsaufnahme der deutschen tv-plattform (2013)
17. de Telecomunicaes (Anatel), A.N.: Tv paga fecha maio de 2013 com 16,93 milhes de assinaturas (2013)
18. Levira: Tdf media services (2014). http://levira.tv/wp-content/uploads/2013/09/Bastian-Manintveld.pdf
19. Soares, L.F.G., Moreno, M.F., De Salles Soares Neto, C.: Ginga-NCL: declarative middleware for multimedia IPTV services. IEEE Communications Magazine **48**(6), 74–81 (2010)
20. Merkel, K.: Hybrid broadcast broadband tv, the new way to a comprehensive tv experience. In: 2011 14th ITG Conference on Electronic Media Technology (CEMT), pp. 1–4. IEEE (2011)
21. Calixto, G.M., Keimel, C., Costa, L., Merkel, K., Zuffo, M.K.: Analysis of coexistence of Ginga and HBBTV in DVB and ISDB-TB. In: 2014 International Conference on Consumer Electronics - Berlin. IEEE (2014)
22. Nixon, L., Thomsen, J.: Using HBBTV and a second screen to link tv programs to related content on the web. In: 2014 IEEE Fourth International Conference on Consumer Electronics - Berlin (ICCE-Berlin), pp. 218–219, September 2014
23. Mikityuk, A., Friedrich, O., Nikutta, R.: HBBTV goes cloud: Decoupling application signaling and application execution in hybrid tv. In: Proceedings of the ACM International Conference on Interactive Experiences for TV and Online Video, TVX 2015, pp. 191–196. ACM, New York (2015)
24. dos Santos, M.R., Calixto, G.M., Costa, L.C.P., Zuffo, M.K.: Interoperability analysis for Ginga-NCL and HBBTV application players. In: 2015 IEEE International Conference on Consumer Electronics (ICCE), pp. 5–6, January 2015

Hypervideo, Augmented Reality on Interactive TV

Antoni Bibiloni$^{(\boxtimes)}$, Miquel Mascaró, Pere Palmer, and Antoni Oliver

Universitat de les Illes Balears – Departamento de Matemáticas e Informática, Laboratorio de Tecnologías de la Información Multimedia, LTIM, Palma de Mallorca, Illes Balears, Spain
{toni.bibiloni,mascport,pere.palmer,antoni.oliver}@uib.es

Abstract. In this paper, an Augmented Reality system for the Interactive and Connected TV is presented through the implementation of a Hypervideo platform. This platform consists of two modules that enable editors and viewers to enjoy an AR experience on current generation Interactive TVs.

Two modules are introduced: the first provides the producers tools to manage the audiovisual content and points of interest, while the other is used by the viewers, in order to play the audiovisual production and obtain additional information about the points of interest that appear on the video.

This work presents an innovative way to mix these three technological concepts: interactive video, augmented reality and connected TV.

Keywords: Augmented reality · HBBTV · Android TV · Smart TV · Hypervideo

1 Introduction

A Hypervideo, or "interactive video" [1], is defined as an audiovisual content stream that is offered to the user with a non-linear navigation. The viewer is able to interact with the content through hyperlinks, which are complemented with other mechanisms, such as searching, additional information, sequence or content skipping, etc. all focused to improve the access to the information and with the goal to bring the viewer from a passive to an active state [2].

When mixing the hypervideo concept with real images, we are approaching to augmented reality (AR) applications. AR is the term used to define a direct or indirect vision of the real world, whose elements are combined with virtual elements to create a mixed reality.

In this paper, the development of an interactive video platform, the Hypervideo Platform, is presented with the objective of delivering an AR experience to the viewer, through current generation Interactive TV solutions, such as HbbTV [3], Android TV [4] or Samsung Smart TV [5], including both processes of authoring and visualizing the Hypervideos.

In the following chapters, following a technological review, the Hypervideo structure is presented, and the process needed to create and view a Hypervideo is shown, as well as the modules developed to enable that are also described in detail. Finally, this paper ends proposing some future work ideas, and the conclusions extracted from doing this work are presented.

© Springer International Publishing Switzerland 2015
M.J. Abásolo and R. Kulesza (Eds.): jAUTI 2014, CCIS 389, pp. 17–31, 2015.
DOI: 10.1007/978-3-319-22656-9_2

2   Technological Situation

One of the first implementations performed of a hypervideo [6], the links between the scenes of the video let the spectator choose the scene change. In successive studies [7], [8], a change in the link behavior is proposed: these can be used to obtain additional information about the content being played at that moment, taking a step towards AR.

The design and evaluation of "Hvet" [9], a hypervideo environment for teaching veterinary surgery, show the potential of these kind of environments in education systems.

The LinkedTV project [10] suggests a hypervideo platform based on industry web and broadcast specifications (HTML, HbbTV), assimilating additional information automatically accessing the data available in the WWW through LinkedData.

The current trend is the interactive media, as interactive image services show, such as Thinglink [11], or interactive video, such as Wirewax [12], although only a few technological platforms that aimed for interactive audiovisual content creation could be detected.

This situation and the lack of hypervideo productions with educative, promotional or informative purposes motivated the creation of this project: specify and develop a platform destined to interactive audiovisual content production, distribution and visualization on current generation TV technologies.

3   The Hypervideo Solution

In this project, a hypervideo solution based on video streaming has been chosen, making use of a triple reality:

- An audiovisual track.
- A collection of points of interest.
- The markers that represent these points of interest over the audiovisual track.

3.1   The Audiovisual Track

First, the real world vision is represented in an indirect way through the visualization via streaming of audiovisual content through the Internet. This video track drives the user through the points of interest (PoI).

The audiovisual content can be made on purpose as well as an existing product can be used, taking into account that it has to represent adequately the points of interest.

3.2   The Collection of Points of Interest

Next, the additional information shown in this hypervideo matches the data collected from the points of interest (PoI) represented in the video track:

- Textual information: name and description.
- Typological information: category.
- Visual information: pictures.
- Complementary information: web page, GPS location.

All this data should be gathered before starting the hypervideo creation, in order to assure a better organization.

3.3   The Markers

Finally, the hyperlinks of our hypervideo approach are also called markers. They are always associated with a point of interest and they accomplish a double function:

- As markers or *hot-spots*, they indicate the point on the screen where a point of interest appears.
- As hyperlinks, they enable the user to browse to the additional information related to a certain point of interest.

4   Hypervideo Platform

In this section, the hypervideo content creation, publishing and visualization platform architecture is presented. As shown in Figure 1, the proposed architecture is composed of two modules that interact with a server, which stores and serves the needed data to create and play hypervideo productions.

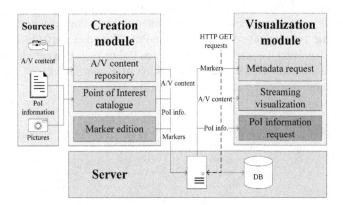

Fig. 1. Hypervideo platform general architecture diagram.

These two modules are described below, and will be further explained in the following sections. In this section, the data model used by the platform is presented, as well as the communications of these modules with the hypervideo server.

4.1   Creation Module

The creation module comprises the tools needed to create a hypervideo, starting by managing the audiovisual repository and inserting new data in the points of interest catalogue.

Once these steps have been completed, the spatiotemporal metadata needed to link the PoIs identified in the media with their markers position is generated.

4.2   Visualization Module

The visualization module is represented by a hypervideo player application, which is able to playback the video track via streaming, represent the markers over it and show the additional information of the chosen points of interest.

A multiplatform development has been followed, being implemented in HbbTV, Android TV and Samsung Smart TV technologies.

4.3   Data Model

The information used by the platform –audiovisual content, points of interest and markers– is stored in a MySQL database, following the data model shown in Figure 2, detailed below:

The *Hypervideo* class stores the basic information to identify and playback the audiovisual content. The *video* attribute contains the video track path to be streamed.

The *Poi* class represents, together with the next two classes, the additional information related with a point of interest. In this class, textual –*name* and *description*– and complementary –*website* and *latitude*, *longitude* and *zoom_lvl*– information is stored.

The *Category* class groups the points of interest according to a certain criteria, representing the typological information of a PoI. The *icon* attribute contains the image used to represent the markers whose related PoI belongs to a certain category.

The *Picture* class stores the visual information of a point of interest. Note that a PoI can have more than one picture.

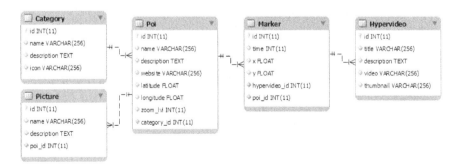

Fig. 2. Hypervideo platform data model.

Finally, the appearances of the points of interest on the hypervideo are expressed in the *Marker* class, pointing out the position (*x,y*) tracking through the lifetime of a marker of a PoI. Also note that the same point of interest can appear independently on multiple hypervideos.

4.4   Server and Module Communication

The hypervideo server acts as an intermediary between the creation and visualization modules with the database. The Apache server gets the HTTP requests of both modules: the first stores the data with HTTP POST requests, while the second gets that data with HTTP GET requests in JSON format.

While the HTTP POST requests from the creation module are pretty straightforward, the HTTP GET requests from the visualization module responses are more complex and are shown next.

Three HTTP GET requests are performed from the visualization module:

- Hypervideo list request
- Hypervideo metadata request
- PoI additional information request

The hypervideo list request response body is encoded in JSON format. The *hypervideoList* key contains an array of hypervideos. Each of these have the properties defined in the data model –*id*, *title*, *description*, *thumbnail* and *video*–.

The *metadata* is the information required to play a hypervideo. In the hypervideo metadata request, the *hypervideo* property defines an object, whose keys can be put in 4 groups:

- Audiovisual content location: *title* and *video* properties.
- Category list: the *categories* property contains an object, whose keys are the identifiers of the categories of the PoIs that appear in the production. For each of these categories, its *name* and *icon* are provided.
- Points of interest and their category: the *pois* key contains an object, whose keys are the identifiers of the PoIs that appear in the production. For each of these points of interest, the identifier of its category is provided.
- Marker tracking: the *markers* key contains an object, whose keys match the seconds where a marker has to be rendered on the screen. For each of these seconds, another object is defined, whose keys are the identifiers of the points of interest that marker represents. For each of these, an object is defined, containing the *x* and *y* properties that specify the point on the screen where the marker has to be rendered.

Finally, the PoI additional information request response body is encoded in JSON format, and as the PoI typological information is already known, the following data is received as properties of the poi key:

- Textual information: *name* and *description* properties.
- Visual information: the *pictures* property defines an array of picture URLs.
- Complementary information: the *website* property contains the PoI webpage URL, which is also encoded in a QR code, using base64 in png format and stored in the *qr* property. The *location* key defines an object, with *latitude*, *longitude* and *zoom_lvl* properties, used to display a map.

5   Creation Module

The goal of this module is enable the user to create hypervideos through three steps: manage the audiovisual content repository, create the point of interest catalogue and edit the placements of the markers.

5.1   Audiovisual Content Repository

In order to guarantee compatibility with the specifications used in the visualization module –HbbTV 1.0 [13], Android [14] and Samsung Smart TV 2012 [15]–, multimedia content must meet the following specification:

- Video codec H264/AVC
- Audio codec HE-AAC
- Container MP4

This multimedia file is uploaded to the platform through the audiovisual repository management interface, enclosing descriptive information about the hypervideo.

5.2   Point of Interest Catalogue

The PoI catalogue is based on categories. First, categories are created as needed through the category management interface, attaching its name and icon.

The category icon must be in PNG format with transparent background, and its size must be 36x72px. In the first half of the image the "inactive" category icon will be placed, while the "active" icon will be placed in the lower half.

Once needed categories are created, the editor inserts the new points of interest in the platform. The form is filled with the PoI data: name and description (textual information), category (typological information), pictures (visual information), web page URL and location, selected with an interactive map (complementary information).

5.3   Marker Edition

The markers purpose is to position the points of interest over the video images. In order to ease the marker edition, a tool inside the creation module is developed and shown in Figure 3.

This tools lets the producer browse the media content, select the temporal intervals where a point of interest appears, and specify its position, pointing out as many key positions as needed.

Fig. 3. Hypervideo marker edition interface.

Once the positions are defined, intermediate positions are generated through lineal interpolation, at a position per second frequency. If it is needed, the editor is able to correct these automatically generated positions.

The result of specifying the markers is stored in the database as the temporal tracking of the markers as a tuple, described in (1): in function of the hypervideo h, the second t and the PoI p, what position (x,y) relative to the video size a marker has.

$$f(h,t,p) = (x,y) \tag{1}$$

6   Visualization Module

The visualization module is represented by the Hypervideo player, developed as a multiplatform application for the following interactive TV technologies: HbbTV 1.0, Android 4.0 and Samsung Smart TV 2012.

These technologies introduce a type of application known as "Web Application" [16] or "Javascript Application" [17] that eases multiplatform development. Having all the TV technologies using similar development model makes it suitable to code a single application logic, with an abstraction layer for every TV technology. The individual web technologies that this module makes use of are shown in Table 1.

Table 1. Web technologies used by Interactive TV.

	Interactive TV technology		
	HbbTV 1.0	**Android WebView**	**Samsung Smart TV**
Markup	CE-HTML [18]	HTML5	
Style	CSS TV Profile 1.0 [19]	CSS3	
Interactivity	ECMAScript (Javascript)	Javascript	

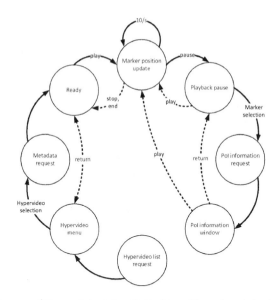

Fig. 4. Sequence diagram of the module states. Dotted transitions denote backwards transitions.

6.1   Application States

The hypervideo player states sequence is shown in Figure 4 and the behavior of the application in each of these states is described next:

In the first state, *hypervideo list request*, an HTTP GET request is done to the server via the XMLHttpRequest object [20]. When the application gets the response, the hypervideo menu is built and the application enters the next state.

In the second state, *hypervideo menu*, the user can select which hypervideo wants to play, heading into the metadata request state.

The application asks the server for the selected hypervideo metadata in the third state, named *metadata request*. This is done as before, through an HTTP GET request via the XMLHttpRequest object. When the reponse arrives to the application, the data structures needed to play the hypervideo are prepared and the application state changes to ready.

The fourth state, *ready*, shows the user that the hypervideo streaming can be played when it presses the play key, entering the next state.

In the fifth state, *marker position update*, the streaming playback is going on while the markers are shown over it. Their position is calculated synchronously via linear interpolation ten times per second, in order to smoothen their movement.

As shown in Figure 5, the current position is calculated from the position for the current second and the position for the following second.

While in the fifth state, the user is able to filter the markers that appear by their category, through the category menu. In order to select a point of interest, following the link of a marker, the user first has to press the *pause* key, entering the next state.

```
t = current_second;
d = current_second % 1;
// for every PoI that is going to appear
p0 = position_in(t);
p1 = position_in(t + 1);
p = {'x': (p1.x - p0.x) * d + p0.x,
     'y': (p1.y - p0.y) * d + p0.y};
```

Fig. 5. Marker position interpolation pseudocode.

In the sixth state, named *playback pause*, the user can select the marker(s) that appear on the hypervideo, if there is any marker. By pressing the *enter* key, the user follows the link denoted by the marker to the point of interest, entering the following state.

The application performs an HTTP GET request to the server in the seventh state, *PoI information request*, through the usual mechanism. When the application gets the response, the point of interest information window is built and the application enters the last state.

In the eighth and last state, *PoI information window*, the additional information of the selected point of interest is shown. The user is able to browse the textual information, as well as the visual information (pictures). The complementary information is shown as a QR-code (website) and a Google Static Map [21] (location).

6.2   User Interface

Player user interface is described in the following figures, showing the different parts of the application, as well as the changes in the interface on state changes.

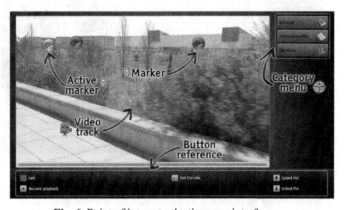

Fig. 6. Point of interest selection user interface.

The interface for states 4, 5 and 6 is shown in Figure 6. It has been divided in three areas: video and markers area, category menu and button reference. In the first area, the markers overlay the video streaming, representing the points of interest that appear in the video. If the user is selecting markers to access their additional information, these appear as "active" markers. On the right, the category menu lets the user filter the markers that appear by their category. Finally, at the bottom, the button reference informs the user of which buttons can it press and what is its function.

When the user gets the additional information of a point of interest, entering the eighth state, that data is arranged in a window, showing the PoI textual information (name, description and website) and a picture, as shown in Figure 7.

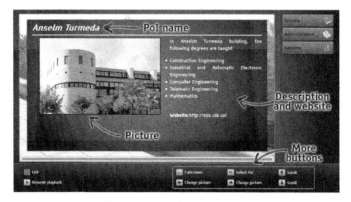

Fig. 7. PoI information window user interface.

The user can navigate through pictures with *left* and *right* buttons, as well as rendering them taking up the entire window by pressing the *enter* key, as described in Figure 8.

Fig. 8. PoI picture full size user interface.

Finally, as represented in Figure 9, the user can get the complementary information in a visual way, navigating across pictures: the point of interest location is shown in a Google Static Maps image and the website URL is encoded in a QR. Both of these images can be displayed taking up the entire window as well.

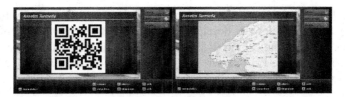

Fig. 9. PoI complementary information user interface.

The user interaction with the interface is done mainly via the remote buttons: the D-pad (*up, right, down, left* and *enter*), the VCR buttons (*play, pause* and *stop*), the *return* button and the *red* button, used to close the application in any state.

In addition to these buttons, the application has been developed bearing in mind the gestures enabled in Samsung Smart TV, displaying a cursor where the user puts its hand, introducing hover, selection and drag in the interface.

6.3   Multiplatform Development

As introduced before, the visualization module has been developed as a web application. In order to make it compatible for HbbTV, Android and Samsung Smart TV it was necessary to introduce an abstraction layer over the application itself for each TV platform.

In the end, each of these versions of the same application will be accessed in different ways: the HbbTV application is hosted in a web server and requested by HbbTV decoders; the Android version is requested from a WebView [22] in an Android application; while the Samsung application is packed in a zip file [23] and uploaded to the Smart Hub.

These abstraction layers are coded as Javascript constructors, named *HbbTV, AndroidTV* and *Samsung*, introducing virtual key definitions (such as *VK_LEFT*, etc), the following methods: *init, addKeyDownListener*, and *exit*, and the constructor *SystemPlayer*, which wraps the behavior of an mp4 streaming player by exporting the following methods: *play, pause, stop, seek, playState, currentState, duration, setOnPlayStateChange* and *setOnPlayPositionChanged*, and the *PLAY_STATES* object.

The HbbTV layer makes use of the elements *video/broadcast* and *application/oipfApplicationManager* present on the DOM, while the *SystemPlayer* introduces an *<object>* element with type *video/mp4* to stream the video.

The Android layer talks with the Java application that contains the *WebView* which is displaying the web app. The communication in Javascript to Java direction is made through the *window.AndroidInterface* object, which shows the method *destroyApplication*; the communication in Java to Javascript direction is obtained via the *window.android* object, whose *keydown* method is called by the Java application when a key is pressed. The *SystemPlayer* introduces an HTML5 *<video>* element to stream the video playback.

Finally, the Samsung layer makes use of the proprietary objects *Common.API.Widget* and *Common.API.TVKeyValue*, while the *SystemPlayer* follows the HTML5 way, just as the Android version.

All this layer choosing work is done by a tool that we built specially for this purpose: *TVmake*. It enables the developer to generate different versions of the same application, by including certain files in each version. It also is able to parse the files to be included with the PHP parser, so in the *<head>* of the *index.html* only the necessary Javascript files are included.

7   Future Work and Conclusion

In this section, a series of future work proposals have been identified and are discussed below. Finally, the conclusion of this work ends the paper.

7.1   Future Work

It has been noticed that during the PoI catalogue creation process, 3rd party information sources are checked in order to complete the PoI addition information. For this reason, and to ease the entire process, we are integrating the creation module with the point of interest database of Open Street Map, accessing its public API [24].

Another aspect that is going to be improved is the marker edition process. The manual model introduced in this paper can lead to mistakes and is a hard task in long videos. In order to automate this process, two techniques have been conceived, depending on the audiovisual content nature:

When working with a multimedia content recorded in the outdoors, with points of interest that can be identified and distinguished with their GPS position, such as buildings, the marker edition can be automated following a location-based process. The camera GPS position and orientation needs to be recorded during the content filming. This data is used together with the volume of the point of interest in GPS coordinates to calculate the viewing frustum (Figure 10), to know if a point of interest appears on the screen and which (x,y) position takes.

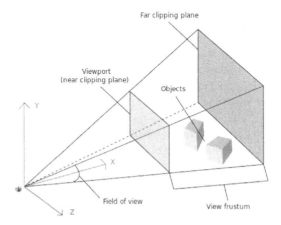

Fig. 10. Viewing frustum to automate the marker positioning.

However, when recording content in the interiors, with steady filming conditions, an alternate technique can be used: object contour detection and shape tracking. Examples of points of interest can be artwork in a museum. In order not to detect every object in the content, a picture of the desired PoIs needs to be supplied.

When applying any of these techniques, a reviewing process has to be introduced so as not to make the user experience worse.

In order to improve user interaction with the audiovisual creations, non-linear hypervideo navigation through their points of interest is presented:

- Intra-hypervideo navigation: a PoI links to a related PoI in the same content, enabling the user to explore other points of interest of the same topic.
- Inter-hypervideo navigation: a PoI links to its apparition in other hypervideo, enabling the user to look into that point of interest from another topic.

Currently, visualization module has been developed in three interactive TV technologies: HbbTV, Android TV and Samsung Smart TV. It is planned to make it compatible with more platforms and devices, such as Internet browsers and tablets, through its implementation in HTML5, iOS and other technologies.

One of the interactive TV technologies used, HbbTV, allows the development of live broadcast-based applications. It is wanted to deliver the audiovisual content through the broadcast channel and enabling marker selection and the PoI information window over it. It is being studied whether to pause the video track when selecting a PoI and then continue via streaming or not doing so, in conjunction with next proposal.

A common trend among interactive TV applications is the introduction of a second-screen application [25]. This application has many different uses, from replacing remote controller to social networking. The requirements for the hypervideo second-screen application are focused on a multi-user model:

- Obtain the additional information of a PoI: the PoI information window will be represented in the mobile application, so as not to disturb other users pausing the video and with additional information of a PoI that is not of their interest.
- Share the additional information of a PoI: the PoI information window goes back to the TV, so a user can share its experiences.
- Complementary information access: the user is able to access the additional information of the PoI directly from its device.
- Social networking: like and share hypervideo content, such as content snapshots or points of interest.

Finally, 360-degree video [26] support is being studied, largely improving user interactivity with the content.

7.2   Clonclusion

The results of the preliminary testing stage between audiovisual producers and university students has been very positive, emphasizing the added value of hypervideo productions destined to educative, promotional or informative purposes. Two key aspects were identified: 1) the importance of the audiovisual sources, revealing the need write down a filming script, listing the points of interest that are wanted to be displayed, and 2) it is essential keeping in mind the user perception in the visualization of a hypervideo: the time interval while the markers are alive has to be long enough to allow the users to see them and these cannot appear too piled up. These aspects ensure the system usability, easing the user to focus on the markers and tell them apart.

A test amongst users, University students, has been very successful, two factors being: 1) the increase in interest for making use of audiovisual content in an interactive way, and 2) the valuation of links between hypervideos, proving that the navigation through topics of interest via the points of interest is accepted and understood by the user.

An in-depth usability study will be conducted in the future, to assess the effectivity, efficiency and satisfaction perceived by users of both modules.

Acknowledgement. This work was supported by project ConTVLab IPT-2012-0871-430000 of the Spanish Government.

References

1. Sawhney, N., Balcom, D., Smith, I.: Hypercafe: narrative and aesthetic properties of hypervideo. In: Proceedings of the Seventh ACM Conference on Hypertext, pp. 1–10 (1996)
2. Landow, G., Kahn,P.: Where's the hypertext? The Dickens web as a system-independent hypertext. In: Proceedings of the ACM conference on Hypertext, pp 149–160 (1992)
3. HbbTV (2014). http://hbbtv.org/. (Accessed: August 1, 2014)
4. Android TV (2014). http://www.android.com/tv/. (Accessed: August 1, 2014)
5. Samsung Smart TV (2014). http://www.samsung.com/smarttv. (Accessed: August 1, 2014)
6. Sawhney, N., Balcom, D., Smith, I.: Authoring and navigating video in space and time. IEEE Multimedia **4**, 30–39 (1997)
7. Doherty, J., et al.: Detail-on-demand hypervideo. In: Proceedings of the 11th ACM International Conference on Multimedia, pp. 600–601 (2003)
8. Shipman, F., Girgensohn, A., Wilcox, L.: Combining spatial and navigational structure in the hyper-hitchcock hypervideo editor. In: Proceedings of the Fourteenth ACM Conference on Hypertext and Hypermedia, pp. 124–125 (2003)
9. Tiellet, C., et al.: Design and evaluation of a hypervideo environment to support veterinary surgery learning. In: Proceedings of the 21st ACM Conference on Hypertext and Hypermedia, pp. 213–222 (2010)
10. Proyecto LinkedTV (2014). http://linkedtv.eu. (Accessed: August 1, 2014)
11. Thinglink (2014). https://thinglink.com/. (Accessed: August 1, 2014)
12. Wirewax (2014). https://wirewax.com/. (Accessed: August 1, 2014)
13. ETSI, HbbTV specification Version 1.0 (2010). http://www.hbbtv.org/pages/about_hbbtv/specification.php. (Accessed: August 1, 2014)
14. Google, Supported Media Formats | Android Developers (2014). http://developer.android.com/guide/appendix/media-formats.html. (Accessed: August 1, 2014)

15. Samsung, Player Specification (2014). http://www.samsungdforum.com/Guide/rel00010/index.html. (Accessed: August 1, 2014)
16. Google, Web Apps | Android Developers (2014). http://developer.android.com/guide/webapps. (Accessed: August 1, 2014)
17. Samsung, Coding Your JavaScript Application (2014). http://www.samsungdforum.com/Guide/art00011/index.html. (Accessed: August 1, 2014)
18. Dees, W., Shrubsole, P.: Web4CE: accessing web-based applications on consumer devices. In: Proceedings of the 16th ACM International Conference on World Wide Web, pp. 1303–1304 (2007)
19. W3C Consortium, CSS TV profile 1.0, W3C Candidate Recommendation (2003). http://www.w3.org/TR/css-tv. (Accessed: August 1, 2014)
20. WHATWG, XMLHttpRequest, Living Standard (2014). http://xhr.spec.whatwg.org/. (Accessed: August 1, 2014)
21. Google, Google Static Maps API V2 (2014). https://developers.google.com/maps/documentation/staticmaps/. (Accessed: August 1, 2014)
22. Google, Building Web Apps in WebView | Android Developers (2014). http://developer.android.com/guide/webapps/webview.html. (Accessed: August 1, 2014)
23. Samsung, Testing Your Application on a TV for 2014 (2014). http://www.samsungdforum.com/Guide/art00121/index.html. (Accessed: August 1, 2014)
24. OpenStreetMap Foundation, OpenStreetMap API v0.6 (2014). http://wiki.openstreetmap.org/wiki/API. (Accessed: August 1, 2014)
25. Courtois, C., D'heer, E.: Second screen applications and tablet users: constellation, awareness, experience, and interest. In: Proceedings of the 10th ACM European Conference on Interactive TV and Video, pp. 153–156 (2012)
26. Kolor, 360° video solotuions (2014). http://www.kolor.com/video. (Accessed: August 1, 2014)

IDTV Development Tools

Marking Up Educational Multimedia Content in IPTV Environments: A Proposal

Angela María Vargas-Arcila[1(✉)], Sandra Baldassarri[2(✉)],
and José Luis Arciniegas Herrera[1(✉)]

[1] Universidad Del Cauca, Popayán, Colombia
{amvargas,jlarci}@unicauca.edu.co
[2] Universidad de Zaragoza, Saragossa, Spain
sandra@unizar.es

Abstract. This paper presents a state of the art concerning the studies related to different services that can be found at educational television and the need to annotate their contents. The bibliographic review carried out allowed to detect the lack of a set of metadata for identifying educational multimedia content in IPTV environments, andtaking into account the existence of content fragments in the same environment which can be reused for educational purposes. Therefore, this paper presents an approach to solve this problem.

Keywords: IPTV · Metadata scheme · Educational content

1   Introduction

Internet Protocol Television (IPTV) is defined as high quality multimedia services (television, video, audio, text, graphics and data) delivered over IP-based broadband networks. Their services, from the end-user perspective, are classified according to the characteristics: distributed content services, interactive services, communication services and others services [1]. Likewise, there are different types of content within which educational contents are intended to influence the viewer knowledge, attitudes and values, furthermore can be used by several types of services listed above to support a broader educational television.

The diversity of possible deployed services in IPTV makes necessary to mark-up, describe and identify the resources they use. For this reason, digital television[1] uses metadata in order to store information to define a resource.

Metadata is information that describes, identifies, explains or defines a resource, in order to make it easier its retrieval, use, or manage. Metadata is known as data about data or information about information [2] [3]. Meanwhile, metadata scheme is a set of metadata elements designed for a specific purpose, such as describing a particular type of information resource [3]. In addition, in IPTV context is possible define metadata as information relating to multimedia content or television resources.

---

[1] Both the traditional digital television (terrestrial, satellite, wired) as IPTV.

© Springer International Publishing Switzerland 2015
M.J. Abásolo and R. Kulesza (Eds.): jAUTI 2014, CCIS 389, pp. 35–48, 2015.
DOI: 10.1007/978-3-319-22656-9_3

Consequently, there are several types of metadata used according to the context (advertising, film, news, music, etc.) to facilitate the classification of resources by content and service providers, as well as optimizing the task performed by IPTV services. For example, in interactive services in charge of relating contents or users with contents, like search or recommendation services, is not possible deliver a concrete response when there are not used metadata according to the context, obtaining noise in the results since the semantic content of the resources is not taken into account [2]. Stuart Weibel y Carl Lagoze, recognized leaders in metadata development, affirm that large-scale adoption of descriptive standards and practices for resources, enhance the discovery of relevant resources in any context where recovery is critical [4].

On the other hand, educational television like IPTV service encompasses a clear context within television where multimedia contents can be an educational resource with new alternatives for education. Despite this, the specifications for metadata generally used on television as TV-Anytime, MPEG-7, EBUCore, and others[5], have been focused on different context distinct from education, for example, film, advertising and news or on the general television context [5]. Therefore, in order to describe an educational content one of the following options is generally chosen:

- Use the specifications to mark-up general audiovisual content. However in this case it would not be possible to identify certain educational features of the resource such as level of learning, student profile, etc.
- Use the specifications designed to describe educational resources on the Web, without regard the particularities of television. Example for the latter option are LOM (Learning Object Metadata or IMS Learning Resource Metadata Specification) [6], CanCore (Canadian Core Learning Resource Metadata Protocol) [7], MLR (Metadata for Learning Resources) [8], among others. However, these rules are not designed to take advantage of the particularities of television as segmentation, for example, an audiovisual content as a TV series, may have educational segments with the possibility of being used for learning processes on TV although the entire series is not considered educational.

In the case of educational television (on IPTV), in which different forms of learning are covered, it is necessary to consider that the contents may be marked not only by the staff who is part of the content provider, but also the user can perform this task playing the role of content provider, more specifically for educational processes involving the teacher.

Considering the different actors that can play the role of creating metadata in an environment of educational television, and the existence of recommendations that force the IPTV architecture be able to support the service provider with the capability of creating or amending the metadata associated with a particular content [9], it is necessary to efficiently generate and maintain metadata using schemes including relevant educational information and allow an accurate contents description, thereby avoiding inconsistencies in the records describing a resource that can hide unwanted information resulting in unpredictable and incomplete search [4].

Therefore, the metadata designed to describe a resource on educational television should be designed taking into account who create the metadata (person who plays the role of content provider or end-user), putting the emphasis on staff marking up the content and not in the technology used to create them, giving the possibility to focus on the marking up content task and not in the application that allows to perform this task.

2   State of The Art

This section provides an overview about the main concepts necessary to understand this document: educational television, metadata and metadata schemes. As well, the study of the most relevant works related to different services of educational television and the need to mark-up their content are presented. These studies have been the basis to detect the shortcomings in this area.

2.1   Educational Television

Traditional educational television is responsible of production, aggregation and delivery of educational contents in order to influence on the knowledge, attitudes and values of the viewer. For this purpose, content and services providers have to educate and train professionals in the production and use of media for educational purposes, and research, develop and propose alternatives to technologically mediated education.

In IPTV context, educational contents can be used by several services defined in the complement number five of ITU-T Y series recommendations [1], especially by those services classifies as distributed content and interactive services, giving rise to a broader educational television. As regards the distributed content services, more exactly in broadcast and on-demand services, the traditional educational television, as initially was conceived, can be presented.

On the other hand, interactive services, specially learning services, are responsible for providing access to interactive content and learning materials through the end-user terminal, or creating educational processes associated with television to expand contents, feature known as t-learning.

T-learning concerns to interactive learning that use digital TV technologies. Some authors define it as a subset of e-learning or convergence between interactive television and e-learning [10]. However, it is not only an adaptation of the techniques of e-learning for interactive television because t-learning is distinguished by the characteristics of television, for example, low screen resolution of most used end-user terminals, simple remote control, and limited features of end-user terminal. These restrictions make learning objects have to be composed mainly of audio and video [11]. For the particular case of IPTV, t-learning offers the following advantages compared to e-learning:

- Ease of use: the handling of the computer tools requires specific and complex skills, while TV provides easy interaction with which people are already familiar.
- Centrality in domestic life: television is part of daily life for users and it influences their routines, interactions, and space and time distribution.
- Lifelong learning: television can provide a timeless education and managed by users.

In this way, teachers' role in the educational process created through television ceases to be centralized, assuming new roles for coordination and support in the process [10], as well as creation, adaptation and mark-up of, that is to say, teachers can play a content provider role. Also, other concepts of education to television can be applied with t-learning, for example, edutainment which refers to education that entertains or "entercation" as referred in the work [11] to the entertainment that educates.

Therefore, we can affirm that educational television encompasses different forms of learning in IPTV, which are able to expand knowledge, experience and capabilities of viewers, and that the main educational component of educational television is audiovisual content.

2.2   Metadata

As it was previously discussed in the introduction, metadata is information that describes, identifies, explains or defines a resource, in order to make it easier its retrieval, use, or manage [2] [3].

Generally, metadata are used to allude to descriptive registers of digital resources which serve to summarize the content of the resource, allow searching or recovery, specify characteristics of ownership, provide information about how to interpret it, detail the conditions of use, and specify the relationships with other resources, etc. Hence, the metadata are the representation of knowledge contained in the digital resource [2].

- Metadata enhance organization and retrieval of information both automated and human form and also promote interoperability of resources [2] [3]. According to the National Information Standards Organization[2], there are three types of metadata [3]:
- Descriptive metadata: describes a resource for purposes such as discovery and identification (for example: title, abstract, author, keywords).
- Structural metadata: indicates how compound objects are put together, for example, how pages are ordered to form chapters.
- Administrative metadata: provides information to help manage a resource (for example: when and how it was created, who can access it) [3].

Metadata can describe a single resource, a collection, or a component part of a larger resource (for example: a segment of video), and can be embedded in a digital resource or it can be stored separately [3]. In IPTV context, metadata have many applications and different features, from merely identifying the content title or information to populate an EPG (Electronic Program Guide) to providing a complete index of different scenes in a movie or providing business rules detailing how the content may be displayed, copied, or sold [9].

---

[2] NISO is a non-profit association accredited by the American National Standards Institute (ANSI). NISO identifies, develops, maintains, and publishes technical standards to manage information.

2.3   Metadata Scheme

Metadata schemes are sets of metadata elements designed for a specific purpose, such as describing a particular type of information resource [3]. They are also known as metadata record [4], metadata structure or metadata model [2].

The relationship between the metadata scheme and the described resource can occur in two ways: embedded in the digital resource or stored separately. Each of these methods has its advantages and disadvantages so when choosing one the size of the implementation of which the scheme will be part and metadata aging time [4] must be taken into account.

Metadata that are part of a scheme are known as elements. The meaning of such elements is known as the semantics of the scheme, and the values assigned to the elements are the content of the scheme. Optionally, metadata schemes can specify representation rules of the content (for example: should be written in capital letters) and allowable content values (for example: terms to be used based on a specific vocabulary).

Metadata schemes are developed for a variety of environments, users and fields, some examples are: Dublin Core, to describe Web resources; MPEG-7, to describe characteristics of audiovisual objects including still pictures, graphics, 3D models, music, audio, speech, video, or multimedia collections; BMF for the relevant information in the television production processes; EBUCore, to describe radio and television content with the minimum necessary information; TV-Anytime, to describe audiovisual content and segments of content; LOM, to describe digital resources used to support learning; METS, to describe complex objects in a digital library; TEI, to mark-up electronic texts (novels, theater plays, poetry); and many others.

Usually, standardized metadata schemes have been subject to changes due to their implementation in different contexts, these modifications are of two types: extensions and profiles. An extension is the addition of elements to an already developed scheme in order to support the description of an information resource of a particular type or subject. Meanwhile, profile is a subset of a metadata scheme, therefore it can constrain the number of elements that will be used, refine element definitions to describe the specific types of resources more accurately, and specify values that an element can take. In this way, an application profile optimizes the scheme for a particular application [3] [4]. A profile also allows mixing metadata from several schemes and optimize them for the particular application of the profile, for example, GEM profile constrain the elements of Dublin Core and at the same define additional elements extending the Dublin Core metadata set for educational use [3].

There are several tools to mark-up resources through a metadata scheme that are classified as: templates, mark-up tools, extractions tools and conversion tools. In first place, templates allow a user to set metadata values into pre-set fields and they will then generate a formatted set of the element attributes and their corresponding values. In second place, mark-up tools structure the metadata attributes and values into the specified scheme language and will then generate a formatted document, these documents are usually XML or SGML files. In third place, extraction tools automatically create metadata from an analysis of the digital resource. These tools are generally limited to textual resources and are considered as an aid to create metadata because the resulting metadata should always be manually reviewed and edited. In fourth place, conversion tools translate one metadata format performed under a metadata scheme to another format corresponding to a different metadata scheme, consequently the similarity between elements of origin and destination schemes affects the need for an additional editing and manually inputting metadata.

Finally, the quality of metadata is a challenge for marking up a resources, so content creators should be trained to understand metadata and to control metadata vocabulary, concepts and tools. In the same way, metadata schemes for a specific audience, extensions and applications profiles, controlled vocabulary and user guides have been developed and refined.

2.4   Related Works

There are several studies related to mark-up educational multimedia content with metadata schemes. Below, the most relevant works found in the literature are presented and discussed:

- *Multimedia application profiles based on standards: a specific case for UNED* [12]: This work presents a review of metadata schemes and available standards to optimize the searches on repositories of multimedia objects specifically related witch education. A detailed state of the art is presented, indicating the available standards, their origin and comparison between them. In the paper, an extension of LOM-ES metadata scheme is proposed, providing some multimedia information obtained from MPEG-7 scheme. So, on the one hand, the extension allows collecting educational information of objects, and on the other hand, gets a good set of information about the multimedia area if that object present multimedia features, this will enable the subsequent management by the user. However, if this approach is implemented in an educational television environment, it may not be the most appropriate because is based on a scheme for marking up educational contents and then adds particularities of other metadata scheme for marking up multimedia resources, but for IPTV environment should be taken as principal scheme which mark-up multimedia content because audiovisual resources are the main element of this context.
- *A Methodology for the Integration of SCORM with TV-Anytime for Achieving Interoperable Digital TV and e-learning Applications* [13]: This work provides a methodology based on the segmentation of digital television programs to facilitate reuse of distinct segments as sharable learning objects (SCO in terms of SCORM). It uses TV-Anytime metadata scheme because it is able to associate metadata with segments and segments groups of audiovisual content, allowing restructure and repurpose an input audiovisual stream to generate alternative consumption and navigation modes. This work states that there is a correspondence between TV-Anytime program segment and a sharable learning object, therefore performs a mapping between the elements of a program segment and the elements of an Item/SCO. However, the paper doesn't provide a detailed explanation of mapping

between schemes. Furthermore, metadata defined by TV-Anytime to describe a segment are constrained to: title, abstract, keywords, related material and credits, thus it doesn't contain elements to describe educational characteristics of content.

- *A study of Metadata design for e-learning Marketplace based on IPTV* [14]: This study defines marketplace based on IPTV as the marketplace for e-learning service between contents supplier and demander through IPTV environment. It also affirms that this marketplace is increasing the interest of e-learning service provider with its interactive media characteristics, therefore this work has designed metadata that can be used for IPTV e-learning services. For these reason, it assumes an interaction of the different actors in the value chain of IPTV as follows: the content provider creates many educational content to the IPTV service provider who recruits viewers in this case will be seen as students, those who in turn give the details of learning through interaction with television and various applications that provider makes use for this purpose, these learning details are managed by a LMS (Learning Management System). Therefore, educational contents are registered in accordance to the characteristics of a LCMS (Learning Content Management System) and in several versions that are mapped to TV-Anytime when they are broadcast. Nevertheless, this work doesn't support the choice of TV-Anytime metadata as a scheme that allows marking up educational multimedia content in television, and also carries out double record of resources description, a record according to e-learning and another according to television, thus the resource mark-up process becomes tedious and furthermore is tested only on a very specific learning system of the work.

- *Personalized TV Services and T-learning Based on TV-Anytime Metadata* [15]: To support personalized broadcasting service and t-learning, this work proposes to use TV-Anytime standard to make an end-to-end prototype system for personalized broadcasting services based on TV-Anytime Phase 1 standard and propose the method to utilize content package in TV-Anytime Phase 2 to develop a T-learning environment. Nevertheless, TV-Anytime doesn't fulfill the particularities of learning systems supported by this environment where it is necessary to relate user profiles with resources that can support learning user and therefore a description of the resources is necessary to allow performing these relationships while taking into account the particularities of television resource metadata.

- *An extension to the ADL SCORM standard to support adaptivity: The t-learning case-study* [16]: This work studies the adaptation possibilities of the SCORM standard and presents an extension to allow adaptivity according to user's characteristics. The values of these adaptation parameters are deduced from the user profile, using inference rules. This paper describes a case study with a service of t-learning, marking up contents with LOM and gets adapted courses to the user's characteristics before he uses the service. Despite this, LOM is not a metadata scheme designed for a television environment, thus it will not be used by content providers in a real environment of educational television, as well as this involving more complex knowledge to the process of marking up a resource.

- *Enhancing TV programmes with additional contents using MPEG-7 segmentation information* [17]: This paper proposes to offer additional contents linked to the segments of TV programmes by means of semantic relations obtained using MPEG-7 segmentation information. This work propose two different application fields: t-learning, and personalized advertising, however, although considers the segmentation of content as an important element of the educational television, MPEG-7 is not a metadata scheme that allows marking up t-learning contents, that is to say, with educational information, for example, learning level.

- *Multiplatform Learning System Based on Interactive Digital Television Technologies, IDTV* [18]: This work presents an IDTV-based learning system which allows different Interactive Television platforms and different final user devices (Television Set, PC, Mobile Phones, Tablets, etc.) to connect and access learning contents, applications and services under the concepts of multiplatform. This paper affirms that t-learning is based on television technologies therefore learning objects are mainly shaped of video. Hence, in order that a video can be converted into valid learning object, it must be enriched with learning activities and with labels that provides the ability to interact with the video through the information about the content, consequently, this study calls learning objects as Learning Objects Based on Interactive Video (OABVI, by its acronym in Spanish). Metadata scheme used in this work is LOM-CO (an application profile of IEEE LOM), however, the only scheme's function is to make the storage easier and classification of OABVI in specialized repositories without regard the ability of reusing educational videos on other television services.

- *DITV-Learning: An Authoring Tool for Learning Digital Object Creation for Interactive Digital Television* [19]: This paper develops a LDO creation tool (LDO, Learning Digital Objects) for interactive digital television in order to allow teachers act like an author of interactive materials without having programming skills. However, this work doesn't consider that the learning objects for the television context must be composed primarily of video, resulting in the construction of LDO composed of a simple menu that allows access to interactive applications without any relation to audiovisual resources. The objective was that LDO reach more places, preserving the principles of e-learning and changing the computer as a display device for the TV. Furthermore, it does not specify standards for marking up content or construction of learning objects.

2.5   Current Gaps

The study and analysis of previous works have enabled us to find the following gaps:

(a) A metadata scheme that describes educational multimedia content and intended to be used in IPTV educational services was not found in the literature. In other words, non metadata scheme that considers the peculiarities of educational content and television could be found.

(b) In literature review there isn't a metadata scheme for educational television environment that considers the technical limitations of the content providers to prepare information about created resources, whereas in the context of educational television, their role can be played by end-user (in the case of intelligent tutoring systems) or by the same company who produces the contents (in the case of traditional educational television).

(c) In the literature there isn't any application profile for educational multimedia television content developed from existing metadata scheme to multimedia television content and optimized for educational content, since television is the main context. The studies that attempted to perform an approximation of a metadata scheme for educational multimedia contents have done the inverse process.

(d) A metadata scheme for educational television content that takes advantage of television's segmentation property which allows learning services reuse more educational resources, was not found.

(e) Literature doesn't discuss an evaluation method for a metadata scheme in order to verify its functionality in the context for which it was designed.

The relations between related works and current gaps are presented in Table 1. The first column contains the work reference and the remaining columns represent the above gaps (correspondingly) and their relation with the works. The relation between a work and a gap can be partial or total.

Table 1. Relation between related works and current gaps.

Work reference	Gaps				
	(a)	(b)	(c)	(d)	(e)
[12]	√√	√√	√√	√√	√√
[13]	√	√√	√√	-	√√
[14]	√	√√	√√	√√	√√
[15]	√	√√	√√	√√	√√
[16]	√√	√√	√√	√√	√√
[17]	√	√√	√√	-	√√
[18]	√√	√√	√√	√√	√√
[19]	√√	√√	√√	√√	√√

- no relation

√ partial relation

√√ total relation

(a) Doesn't consider the peculiarities of educational content and television.

(b) Doesn't consider the technical limitations of the user who marking up the contents.

(c) Is not developed from existing metadata scheme to multimedia television content and optimized for educational content.

(d) Doesn't take advantage of television's segmentation property.

(e) Doesn't discuss an evaluation method for the metadata scheme.

3   Metadata for Educational Multimedia Content

Previous gaps reflect the following problem: a set of metadata to identify educational multimedia content in IPTV environments and to consider the existence of content fragments contained in the same environment, which can be reused for educational purposes, has not been found.

3.1   Justifications to Solve the Problem

This problem it is important to solve for the below reasons:

- Not always the IPTV services with educational objectives are provided by specialized companies in education or marking up content. In some educational processes the end-user plays that role. In consequence the metadata to mark-up resources should be well specified.
- A well-defined and appropriated set of metadata to describe the context educational television in order to develop IPTV services that make use of audiovisual resource as the main educational component.
- The educational contents could be reused as educational resources, provided that they have a correct description.
- It would encourage the development of future educational services where content-user relationship is important because the content description may be related to the learning level of the user or other user features regarded as a student.
- The value of information depends to a great extent on how easy it is to find, retrieve, manage and access, hence, the accurate content description is a problem that has constantly been researched [20].
- T-learning is based on the experiences of the evolution of e-learning, therefore is important avoid the problems presented in the beginning of t-learning such as the lack of standardization (including the standardization of metadata), as a result of these problems, educational resources can only be used by some educational environment for which they were designed, for example: a description of a resource on Moodle learning platform would not serve to describe the same resource on Caroline learning platform [20].

3.2   Proposal Solution

We propose to design a metadata scheme for marking up IPTV educational multimedia content able to describe educational contents or educational segments of content in that environment.

As Fig. 1 indicates, our design involves three phases: exploration, adaptation and verification.

First, the exploration phase focuses on the study of both existing metadata schemes for marking up multimedia contents and educational contents, so we can define a set of relevant features from the two groups of schemes, so they must be taken into account for the final solution. In this step classification schemes is also obtained and the relationships between them (is profile of, is extension of, arise from, etc.).

Secondly, adaptation phase refers to the selection of existing metadata scheme for multimedia contents that will be taken as the kernel for the creation of the new scheme. The main selection criteria must be: use in digital television environments (has the scheme employed for marking up contents in television environments?), segment description (does the scheme enable to describe segment of contents?), metadata for educational features (does the scheme contain elements for describing educational features of the resource?), possibility of extension or constrain (is it possible to extend or constrain the schema according to a context?) and available documentation (is it easily found technical and theoretical schema documentation?). Also, this phase must identify the metadata required to mark-up contents in educational television environments, through mappings between the most relevant metadata schemes for educational content and the selected scheme. Finally, incorporate such metadata scheme and if necessary, limit or refine it according to the context.

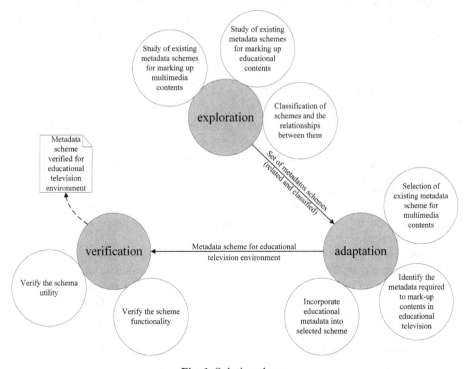

Fig. 1. Solution phases

Third, we verify that the proposed scheme allows the description of educational multimedia content (the schema utility) and furthermore positively influences on an IPTV educational service (the scheme functionality).

The utility of the scheme will be measured through user interaction with marking up content prototype, considering usability issues because the mark-up process is performed by users therefore their perception assess the usefulness of the solution (easy to learn, easy to mark-up, easy to understand, contains sufficient metadata for marking up).

The functionality of the scheme will be measured by evaluating the behavior of an IPTV educational service when the contents are identified with the metadata scheme proposed. At this point and in representation of diverse applications that have a metadata scheme for IPTV educational multimedia, a scenario where educational audiovisual content will be shared between different users using a search service, these contents will be described by teachers experts in the topics covered by resources, and assuming that these teachers are part of a work team of a content provider to mark-up or otherwise they are independent content creators. Is necessary to emphasize that may exist content with educational segments which may also be marked with educational information. Meanwhile, the search service allows to search educational contents in one area of interest to both students and teachers. Thus, the metadata schema to propose, first seeks to be useful for teachers when they describe contents, and reuse existing contents or segments of content, secondly, the usefulness for students will be reflected in the behavior of educational services (adequate searching, accurate recommendations, etc.).

4   Conclusions

This paper presents a review of different studies related to educational television and marking up its contents, which has detected the absence of a metadata scheme or application profile to describe educational multimedia content used by IPTV educational services, that considers the segmentation property of audiovisual resources and also easy to understand for who marking up contents.

A proposal is presented to contribute to solve this problem which aims to propose a metadata scheme for IPTV educational multimedia content, based on a metadata schema as a kernel.

The process to design the metadata scheme is based on three phases: exploration (study of existing metadata schemes, both for marking up multimedia and educational content), adaptation (selection of a metadata schema as a kernel and its modification according to the context of educational television) and verification (utility and functionality test of the proposed metadata scheme).

Acknowledgements. This work is supported by UsabiliTV project (Framework para la evaluación desde la perspectiva de usabilidad de los servicios para soportar procesos educativos en entornos de televisión digital interactiva. ID 1103 521 28462) financed by Education Ministry of Colombia through Colciencias, and executed by Universidad del Cauca. It is also partially financed by the RedAUTI project: Red temática en Aplicaciones y Usabilidad de la Televisión digital Interactiva, CYTED 512RT0461, and the government of Spain through contract DGCYT TIN2011-24660.

References

1. International Telecommunication Union ITU-T, "Supplement on IPTV service use cases", ITU-T Y-series Recommendations – Supplement 5, Mayo de 2008
2. Martínez-Usero, J.A.: El uso de metadatos para mejorar la interoperabilidad del conocimiento en los servicios de ad-ministración electrónica. El profesional de la información 15(2), 114–126 (2006)
3. N. I. S. O. NISO. Understanding metadata. Technical report, National Information Standards Organization NISO (2004)
4. Dublin Core Metadata Initiative DCMI. Guía de uso del Dublin Core, Recurso Recomendado de la DCMI, Agosto 2003
5. NoTube Project, "NoTube", NoTube. [En línea]. Página del proyecto: http://notube.tv/
6. IMS Global Learning Consortium, Inc. Learning resource metadata specification. [En línea]. Página del proyecto: http://www.imsglobal.org/metadata/
7. C. M. Initiative. Cancore. [En línea]. Página del proyecto: http://cancore.athabascau.ca/en/
8. Betrián, D.P., Hilera, J.R., Pagés-Arévalo, C.: ISO/IEC 19788 MLR: Un nuevo estándar de metadatos para recursos educativos. IEEE-RITA 6(3), 140–145 (2011)
9. Unión Internacional de Telecomunicaciones UIT-T Comisión de Estudio 13. Recomendación UIT-T Y.1901 requisitos para los servicios de TVIP, Enero 2009
10. Pindado, J.: T-learning. el potencial educativo de la televisión digital interactiva. In: de Sevilla, U. (ed) Alfabetización mediática y culturas digitales, chapter Capítulo 2: televisión y competencias digitales (I) (2010)
11. Rey-López, M., Díaz-Redondo, R.P., Fernández-Vilas, A., Pazos-Arias, J.J.: Entercation: Engaging viewers in education through TV. ACM Comput. Entertain. 5(2), April 2007
12. Leal, J.L.D.: Perfiles de aplicación multimedia basado en estándares: un caso concreto para la UNED (in Spanish). Asociación Española para la Inteligencia Artificial (AEPIA) (2010)
13. Frantzi, M., Moumoutzis, N., Christodoulakis, S.: A methodology for the integration of SCORM with TV-Anytime for achieving interoperable digital TV and e-learning applications. In: 2004 Proceedings of the IEEE International Conference on Advanced Learning Technologies, pp. 636–638, August 2004
14. Kwon, B.-I., Moon, N.-M.: A study of metadata design for e-learning marketplace based on IPTV. In: Proceedings of the 2009 International Conference on Hybrid Information Technology, ICHIT 2009, pp 79–85. ACM, New York (2009)
15. Lee, H.-K., Yang, S.-J., Lee, H.-K., Hong, J.-W.: Personalized TV Services and T-Learning Based on TV-Anytime Metadata. In: Ho, Y.-S., Kim, H.-J. (eds.) PCM 2005. LNCS, vol. 3767, pp. 212–223. Springer, Heidelberg (2005)
16. Rey-López, M., Díaz-Redondo, R.P., Fernández-Vilas, A., Pazos-Arias, J.J., García-Duque, J., Gil-Solla, A., Ramos-Cabrer, M.: An extension to the ADL SCORM standard to support adaptivity: The t-learning case-study. Comput. Stand. Interfaces 31(2), 309–318 (2009)
17. Rey-López, M., Fernández-Vilas, A., Díaz-Redondo, R.P., López-Nores, M., Pazos-Arias, J.J., Gil-Solla, A., Ramos-Cabrer, M., García-Duque, J.: Enhancing TV programmes with additional contents using MPEG-7 segmentation information. Expert Systems with Applications 37(2), 1124–1133 (2010)

18. Montoya, E., Montoya, J., Téllez, J., Ruiz, C., Vélez, J., Ibarra, O.: Multiplatform learning system based on interactive digital television technologies, IDTV. In: Informatica (CLEI), 2012 XXXVIII Conferencia Latinoamericana En, pp. 1–10, October 2012
19. de Sousa Neto, F.A., Bezerra, E.P.: DITV-Learning: UmaFerramenta de Autoria à Criação de Objetos Digitais de Aprendizagem para Televisão Digital Interativa(in Portuguese). In: Anais do 23° Simposio Brasileiro de Informatica na Educação (SBIE 2012), Novembro 2012
20. Rey-López, M.: PhD thesis, Universidad de Vigo, España (2009)

Application of the I-Standardization in the Production and Management of Current Digital News Reporting: Integration into Broadcast Formats

Miguel Angel Rodrigo Alonso[✉] and Carlos de Castro Lozano

EATCO Research Group, University of Córdoba, Córdoba (España), Spain
miguelangelrodrigo@gmail.com, carlos@uco.es

Abstract. The information society and technological advances have a direct influence on the flow of output of current information, while undergoing various modifications to adapt to these changes. After applying different research methodologies the results indicate that in order to be able to make such adjustment features and meet the demands of end users one needs an optimum level of accessibility and usability in such a workflow with information. As a possible solution to these results the use of the I-standardization is proposed, both as devices and as sources of information used by the producer of digital newspaper content. The design of this process is focused on user requirements; therefore, regulations have been used for a user-centered (DCU) as ISO 13407. Not only are levels of usability and accessibility improved, but also an adaptive final product to various platforms and applications (Moodle, HTML5, MXF, AAF, etc.) is provided. Thus we not only achieve that the use of current information can be integrated, among other things, for use in media and ubiquitous learning environments, but we also will have a greater degree of accessibility and usability in production flow.

Keywords: Usability · Accessibility · Information management · Broadcast · Mxf · I-Standardization · Information sources · Metadata

1   Introduction

The exponential growth of new technologies makes the information model adapt to this pace, creating a metamorphosis from production and transmission to consumption. But, are we properly adapting such information to this progress? Does the information have accessibility and usability?

One of the problems that the professional faces is the increasing demand for information, especially in digital content. This leads to producing more information in the same period of time than was previously produced . If this increase in production has the same tools, the quality of information may be impaired regardless of the efforts of the content producer. It is inevitable at this point to ask whether or not there exists a problem of accessibility and / or usability of the hardware and software in these tools. The language is becoming less developed and fine-tuned linguistically, and tends to produce poor communication. Following these approaches, the EATCO [1] group of

© Springer International Publishing Switzerland 2015
M.J. Abásolo and R. Kulesza (Eds.): jAUTI 2014, CCIS 389, pp. 49–58, 2015.
DOI: 10.1007/978-3-319-22656-9_4

the University of Córdoba [2] has carried out research in recent years, in collaboration with media and professional associations. Research methodologies included surveys, participant observation and personal interviews statewide.

This study showed several results, such as:
• The degree of usability and accessibility of information and production tools are closely linked to the quality and quantity of current information.
• I-Standardization [3] is proposed as a tool for optimizing such degrees. See Figure 1.

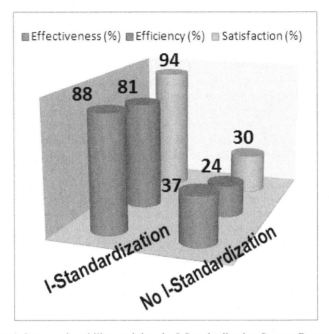

Fig. 1. Improved usability applying the I-Standardization.Source: Prepared

From this, several lines of research were opened. Among them, the use of current information for ubiquitous learning environments and media.

Ubiquity is a quality that occurs every day as a steadily increasing need and demand, not only from the perspective of news production or consumption, but also learning or technology. It is a social need. [4]

2   Inclusion of I- Standardized Information in Format Broadcast

2.1   Using the I-Standardization

To study the degree of accessibility and usability of current information we will have to review carefully the flow in its development. We can differentiate two parts, the sources of information and the subsequent production. The producer of digital news content[1] (PDNC) receives such information from its sources and then develops a product that is inserted into the learning environment.

There are two types of I-Standardization:

• I-Standardization of devices.
The I-Standardization of devices is based on the formal reduction of the number of devices used at a given point in the flow of information and applications available. Its ideal goal is the unification of all hardware and software in a single device.
This device will have an optimum level of accessibility and usability when accessing information. [5]
• I-Standardization of information content.
The I-standardization of information content is based on performing a unified format that comes from information sources. The final format must have the widest possible support for the integration process of cataloging. In the process of reformatting a set of characters that identify the source will be inserted into the message header.

Applying the I-Standardization of information sources and tools used by the producer of digital content generates, on the one hand, an increase in the quality and contrast of the information feedstock as well as speed for the professional who subsequently will give a personal touch of preparation for delivery to the learning environment, and on the other hand, the latter is given the possibility of higher quality and quantity of information messages. If we get an acceptable level of accessibility and usability sources, we save access and contrast time, which in the following parts of the flow can be reversed to reduce the time of insertion of material into the environment or allow more time for the producer to produce a higher quality content.

Besides the above the I-Standardization also provides solutions to other problems:

• If there is a demand for information for consumption, at present, the producer is forced to increase the amount of material produced in compromising quality. If the I-standardization is applied to both sources and production tools we can optimize aspects of usability and accessibility, making the work of the producer more comfortable and efficient.
• Low quality information content. The consumers of information are in the situation where, in order to meet their own demands for a product wherever they may be, they are subjected to an overflow of information of dubious contrast and poor content. Therefore, by integrating the I-standardization, the possibility of a percentage increase in the guarantee of quality and quantity of reception of multimedia learning objects increases.
• Increased sources of information systems. For the process of developing content the producer will survey each of the sources that are received, in addition to various protocols for obtaining it. This creates a delay in the creation of their product, and therefore a time delay.

---

[1] In spanish, PCPD, productor de contenidos digitales.

The I-Standardization processes are focused on user centered (DCU) design. Within the ISO 9241 [6] and its four activities that assess the degree of accessibility, I found your update ISO 13407 [7], adapting to information flow in the current environment. As we can see in Figure 2 it will allow us to measure the effectiveness, efficiency and speed with which information can achieve a certain degree of knowledge of content, a particular group of users and a certain place of delivery, always with the user-centered design, catering to the needs of the same. Although the possibility of using the metric of ISO 9126-1 [8] provided by some publications [9] it was finally dismissed as it seeks a design focused on user requirements, therefore we will continue to use the rules ISO 13407.

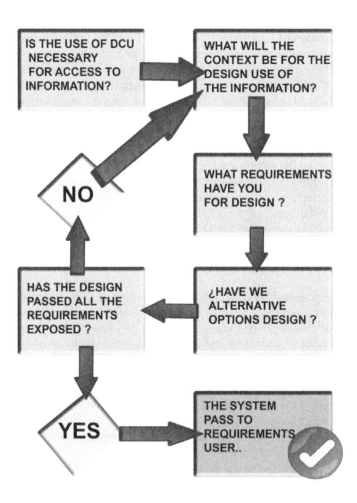

Fig. 2. Application of the standard 13407 the use of information. Source: Prepared

Once the operation of the I-standardization is exposed, what matters is what will show us the exit. Formats on offer are plain text and / or XML. Here we see an example of the output of I-standardized information whose origin is from a spanish teletype information agency:

```xml
<?xml version="1.0" encoding="UTF-8"?>
<Pnews xmlns:xsi="http://www.w3.org/2001/XMLSchema-
instance">
  <HeadInfo>
    <AssetID>13091801221439423</AssetID>
    <SourceID>t1tipo</SourceID>
    <SourceTags>SOC</SourceTags>
  </HeadInfo>
  <HolderInfo> Detenidas 15 personas por presuntamente
cultivar y elaborar marihuana, tras intervenir más de 50
kilos</HolderInfo>
  <TextInfo> En un comunicado, la Benemérita ha informado
de que, dentro del marco de los servicios establecidos en
aplicación de la Operación 'Marihuana' para la
"erradicación" del cultivo, elaboración, venta y consumo
de marihuana, ha practicado en las últimas semanas, en
concreto entre los días 15 al 24 de septiembre, un total
de 12 intervenciones que han permitido detener a 15
personas por cultivo y elaboración de marihuana.Como
resultado de estos 12 operativos, el Instituto Armado,
además de las 15 detenciones practicadas, ha logrado
aprehender 46 plantas de marihuana en fase de
crecimiento, que tras su pesaje arrojaron un peso de más
de 50 kilogramos. </TextInfo>
</Pnews>
```

As to the utility of the labels we have three structures:

- *HeadInfo* is what we call header data, which houses other labels classifying information as *AssetID*, identification and classification for use of the file *SourceID*, which indicates which is the source (tickers, sms, fax, etc. .) and finally, *SourceTags*, showing us the keywords or tags that define the theme of the i-standardized information.
- *HolderInfo* includes the news headline.
- *TextInfo* contains all the information developed.

2.2 Integration of I-Standardized Information as MXF and AAF Metadata Formats

MXF (Material Exchange Format) [10] is a file format aimed at exchanging audiovisual material with associated metadata between applications. Its technical characteristics are defined in SMPTE 377m [11] standard and was developed by the Pro-MPEG Forum, the EBU organization and the AAF Association, together with leading companies and manufacturers in the broadcast industry. The ultimate goal is an open file format that facilitates the sharing of video, audio, data and associated metadata within a workflow based on files.

An MXF file is a container that can carry video, audio, graphics, etc. and its associated metadata, in addition to the necessary information that forms the structure of the file metadata.

An important factor is that MXF is independent of the compression format used because it can carry different types of formats like MPEG, DV or sequence of TIFFs. The great advantage of MXF is that it allows saving and exchanging associated metadata that describes the content and the way in which the file should be read.

Metadata may contain information on:

- File structure
- The content itself (MPEG, DV, ProRes, DNxHD, JPG, PCM, etc.)
- Timecode
- Keywords or titles
- Subtitles
- Release Notes
- Date and version

MXF is based on the model of AAF (Advanced Authoring Format) data and are complementary to each other. The difference is that the AAF format is optimized for post production processes, because it allows storing a larger number of metadata and enables using references to external materials. The MXF files can be embedded within the AAF files, which means that an AAF project may include audiovisual content and associated metadata, but can also call other MXF content hosted externally.

Achieving greater compatibility is the main objective of MXF and three areas are established:

-*Multiplatform*. It may work in different network protocols and operating systems, including Windows, Mac OS, Unix and Linux.
Independent
 -*Compression*. It offers easy handling of more than one native format. Plus you get to handle the uncompressed video.
-*Transference streaming*. You can set a bidirectionality transfer (sending / receiving files MXF).

A MXF file has a structure that houses a header file where the content and timing are detailed, the metadata associated with multimedia content, the body that contains the original multimedia data and tail closes the file. The data in MXF files are encapsulated using subdivisions called threesome of values KLV (Key-Length-Value). This contains a unique identification key (Key) of 16 bytes for each triplet, the value of the length (Length) of the data stored in the threesome and if data (value). With this data organization enables us to locate any specific element within the MXF file by just reading the keys of identification. It also allows the file format to grow and add new features with new compression techniques and metadata schemes.

You can go a little further. Let's look at *Figure 3* because partitions are allowed within a KLV. A threesome may be fragmented in a succession of KLV and yields greater stability to the file structure. For example, if we send a MXF file over the network and a connection loss should occur, and therefore the file transfer fails, when the connection is restored there is no need to resubmit the entire file but one can initiate the transfer in the threesome where it is short.

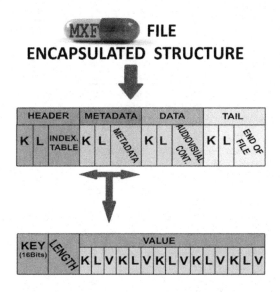

Fig. 3. MXF File encapsulated structure Source: Prepared

In order to integrate the metadata you get on I-standardization in an MXF file in the metadata, we use a scheduled C application called MXFwrapper.c, which will hold an encapsulated metadata. The execution of this application will be done with the following commands:

```
Mxfwrapper <fichero.xml> <fichero.mxf>
```

We find the problem that generates MXF XDCAM camcorder file is not compatible with other manufacturer MXF file generated in their models Panasonic P2. The flexibility of the MXF feature allows the offer of different applications and options to the rule by various different manufacturers, because of which there are MXF that are not compatible between manufacturers. This lack of standardization has led to implementing a number of different physical versions for improved compatibility based on their applications. Thus, so-called operational patterns have been established and each will have its own specifications under a standard that defines the type of image, sound and metadata sets.

One solution is the OP-Atom. It is a very simple file format that can only be essentially a single element, either a video track or audio. Usually, the metadata associated with the media containing OP-Atom MXF file is in XML or AAF. To finish, an executable has been created, able to integrate the content of the XML file off of I-standardization in XML of an MXF OP-Atom Finally, as we can see in the following example ClipMetadata content of an XML tag P2:

```
<P2Main>
|
|
|
<ClipMetadata>
    |
    |
    | <Access>
        <CreationDate>2013-08-12T11:13:37+01:00</CreationDate>
        <LastUpdateDate>2013-08-12T11:13:37+02:00</LastUpdateDate>
        <LastUpdatePerson>ingesta</LastUpdatePerson>
    </Access>

    <Shoot>
        <StartDate>2013-08-12T11:13:37+01:00</StartDate>
        <EndDate>2013-08-12T11:13:37+01:00</EndDate>
    </Shoot>
    <Thumbnail>
        <FrameOffset>0</FrameOffset>
        <ThumbnailFormat>BMP</ThumbnailFormat>
        <Width>80</Width>
        <Height>60</Height>
    </Thumbnail>
    <News>
        <HeadInfo>
         <AssetID>130918</AssetID>
        <SourceID>t1tipo</SourceID>
        <SourceTags>SOC</SourceTags>
        </HeadInfo>
    <HolderInfo> Detenidas 15 personas por presuntamente
     cultivar y elaborar marihuana, tras intervenir más de 50 kilos</HolderInfo>
    <TextInfo> En un comunicado, la Benemérita ha informado de que,
     dentro del marco de los servicios establecidos en aplicación de la Operación
     'Marihuana' para la "erradicación" del cultivo, elaboración, venta y consumo de marihuana,
     ha practicado en las últimas semanas, en concreto entre los días 15 al 24 de septiembre,
     un total de 12 intervenciones que han permitido detener a 15 personas por cultivo
     y elaboración de marihuana.Como resultado de estos 12 operativos, el Instituto Armado,
     además de las 15 detenciones practicadas, ha logrado aprehender 46 plantas de marihuana
     en fase de crecimiento, que tras su pesaje arrojaron un peso de más de 50 kilogramos.
    </TextInfo>
        </News>
    </ClipMetadata>
    </ClipContent>
</P2Main>
```

3   Conclusions

Current information is a great resource that any community should have in order to develop. Therefore, information and education are fundamental human rights for people and their freedom [12].

The I-Standardization is a key to increasing degrees of usability and accessibility of information tool. Therefore, the integration of an i-standardized information product, has advantages such as:

- The possibility of increased quality of content.
- Higher degree of immediacy of delivery of the final information product to the user.
- Increased accuracy in controlling information sources.
- Adaptability to new platforms or future media formats of higher quality thanks to encapsulated MXF.
- By having information integrated in the MXF metadata it gives us a backup or backup information.
- We obtain greater usability and accessibility having a single file containing the average, i-standardised information and the possibility of inclusion of other accessible elements such as subtitles.

In previous workshops the use of i-standardized information was presented within ubiquitous learning systems [13] [14] which could be justified from the results of the pedagogical and technological relationship, which has not been analyzed in previous studies [15].

Another use of the I-Standardization has been put forward, offering a description of the process of wrapper, the XML i-standardized file in MXF encapsulated. Therefore, the idea and justified advantages of using the i-standardized information as part of the metadata exchange of audiovisual material in companies or media has been contributed.

We have managed to establish a theoretical and practical basis for the implementation of future international research projects for the application of current information in the areas that are exposed or in others that can be considered viable.

References

1. Grupo de investigación EATCO. http://eatco.es/index.php/productos-y-servicios
2. De Castro Lozano, C.: El futuro de las tecnologías digitales aplicadas al aprendizaje de personas con necesidades educativas. Revista de Educación a Distancia, 2 y 31. Universidad de Murcia (2012). www.um.es/ead/red/32/carlos.pdf
3. Alonso, R., Ángel, M.: Tesis: Perfil del Productor de Contenidos Periodísticos Digitales y sus herramientas de gestión. Influencia, usabilidad y accesibilidad a nuevas Tics. El caso de Córdoba (España). Universidad de Córdoba. Córdoba (2014)

4. Zapata Ros, M.: Calidad en entornos ubicuos de aprendizaje. Revista de Educación a Distancia. Universidad de Murcia, p. 5 (2012). http://www.redalyc.org/articulo.oa?id= 54723302004
5. Rodrigo, M.A., De Castro, C.: La información digital actual, un nuevo modelo de contenido educativo para un entorno de aprendizaje ubicuo. RED, Revista de Educación a Distancia. Núm. 39. ISSN 1578-7680 (2013). http://www.redalyc.org/articulo.oa?id= 54729539002
6. ISO 9241-210:2010. http://www.iso.org/iso/catalogue_detail.htm?csnumber=52075
7. ISO 13407. http://www.ucc.ie/hfrg/emmus/methods/iso.html
8. NC-ISO-IEC 9126-1. Parte 1. Modelo de Calidad. Oficina Nacional de Normalización, ONN (2005)
9. León Perdomo, Y., Enrique Góngora Rodríguez, A., Febles Estrada, A.: Aplicando métricas de calidad a proyectos y procesos durante las pruebas exploratorias. Revista Cubana de Ciencias Informáticas 7(2), Abril-Junio, 2013
10. MXF. http://en.wikipedia.org/wiki/Material_Exchange_Format
11. SMPTE 377M. http://read.pudn.com/downloads166/doc/fileformat/759223/mxf/SMPTE% 20377M-2003%20Television%20Material%20Exchange%20Format%20%28MXF%29% 20File%20Format%20Specification%20%28Standard%29%5BP1.PDF
12. Freire, P.: La educación como práctica de la libertad. Ed. Siglo XXI (2007)
13. Alonso, M.A.R.: La información digital, un nuevo modelo de contenido educativo para un entorno de aprendizaje ubicuo. In: II Jornadas Iberoamericanas sobre aplicaciones y usabilidad de la TV Digital. Redauti. Universidad de Córdoba, Septiembre 2013. http://jauti 2013.cpmti.es/AlonsodeCastro.pdf
14. Ogata, H., Yano, Y.: Knowledge awareness map for computer-supported ubiquitous language-learning, pp. 19–23 (2004)
15. Gros, B.: Retos y tendencias sobre el futuro de la investigación acerca del aprendizaje con tecnologías digitales. Revista de Educación a Distancia 4. Universidad de Murcia (2012). http://www.redalyc.org/articulo.oa?id=54724591003

IDTV Evaluation and Testing

A Software Testing Process for Ginga Products

Gabriella Alves[(⊠)], Rennan Barbosa, Raoni Kulesza, and Guido L.S. Filho

NPE-LAVID/UFPB, Cidade Universitária, Campus I, João Pessoa, PB 58059-900, Brazil
{gabriellalves,rennan,raoni,guido}@lavid.ufpb.br

Abstract. The objective of this work is to define and evaluate the process of software testing development for the Ginga platform, focusing on system testing specifically for Ginga-NCL. The main motivations are Brazil's expectation has 54 million TV sets with Ginga by the end of 2016 and the lack of systematic approaches to software testing for these products. The proposed process is divided into planning, specification, implementation and analysis. This paper presents an assessment of all steps from the execution of tasks, papers and generating artifacts using products on the market today in a production environment.

Keywords: Development process · Software test · Digital TV · Ginga

1   Introduction

The transition from analog TV to digital TV has been taking place in various parts of the world. In Brazil the first steps towards the implementation of Digital TV were performed in 2005 with the creation of the Brazilian Digital TV System (SBTVD), which provides some innovations, such as interactivity, through the middleware Ginga, divided into two subsystems, the Ginga-J execution environment (procedural) and presentation environment Ginga NCL (declarative).

According to the Ministry of Communications of Brazil, there are between 60 and 80 million analog devices in operation a total population of 54 million households. Of these, 16 million families are "class" D and E, and represent 30% of the population that use TV as the primary means of information and entertainment. Currently, the digital signal reaches 25 states of Brazil, with only 2 states (Amapá and Roraima) without transmissions. Of the 5509 municipalities, only 433 have coverage of the digital signal. Though coverage 45.5% of the population, access of Brazilians to the digital signal is still far from universal, whether in fixed or mobile reception. However, with the Interministerial Ordinance 140, published on February 23, 2012, which requires that manufacturers include Ginga in 75% of TV sets in 2013 and 90% in 2014, it is expected that this market could reach 54 million interactions with devices by the end of 2016, making it equivalent in quantity to the smartphone market in the country.

Given this expected expansion implementation of the Ginga platform, there is a need for system quality assurance. Therefore, the test activity becomes a critical task in the final product development process support system as reliability, since it is

© Springer International Publishing Switzerland 2015
M.J. Abásolo and R. Kulesza (Eds.): jAUTI 2014, CCIS 389, pp. 61–73, 2015.
DOI: 10.1007/978-3-319-22656-9_5

adopted a test procedure in which their activities are conducted in an objective manner and arranged. Software testing process defines how the tests are planned, designed, implemented, executed and evaluated through a set of activities, artifacts and roles [1]. A typical process includes a set of activities such as: (1) planning, determines what, how, when, and by whom will be held; (2) specification, creates the artifacts relating them with the features that will be covered; (3) implementation, implements the code required to run the test; and (4) analysis, conducts a survey of the application of tests.

This paper proposes a software testing process for evaluating the Ginga platform, specifically for the subsystem Ginga-NCL, responsible for the implementation of NCL declarative app. Furthermore, the development of this process is based on software testing documents provided by the IEEE 829 standard [2] consisting of a set of documents to be produced along the activities of the proposed process. The main objective is to define and evaluate a software testing process for Ginga platform, emphasizing the Ginga-NCL, ensuring the quality of a final product.

The organization's work is: the next section talks about related work. The third section explains the basics of software testing under the proposal of this work. The fourth section describes the proposed test methodology. The fifth shows the methodology of assessments using Ginga-NCL products. The discusses the conclusions and future work.

2   Related Work

Currently, the scientific community there is research work dealing with digital TV middleware for testing process. The following are the paper that has more proximity to our work.

UniSoft Corporation [3] is a software company specializing in the supply of transmission tools, software development and specific tests for interactive TV standards, located in the United States. Its test development strategy uses the standard test suites, especially for API testing, where the assertions are based on testing techniques. The test assertions (also known as a description of the test) are formed by details of an individual unit of functionality or behavior derived from information contained in the specification of APIs to be tested. In their software development methods applied in the projects, check: (i) a statement of work; (ii) development of the test plan; (iii) generation of assertions; (iv) generation of test case strategies; (v) generation test code; and (vi) test system.

The MHP-CONFIDENCE (MHP - Conformance Testing Improvement by Development of New Conformance Tests in Europe) [4] is a project related to the MHP, which aims to strengthen the development and improvement of test cases to use the official test scheme DVB compliance as part of the official test suite implementations. The main activities that the MHP CONFIDENCE adopted for the development of systems are identification, specification, creation and verification of compliance tests. These validation tests are available through the standardization process of the DVB and ETSI (European Telecommunications Standards Institute), as an additional part of the official test suite of MHP.

Works as Unisoft and MHP-CONFIDENCE have focused on system testing and use paid tools. Their main difference related to the proposed work is the need for active participation as a member of the development team of a project or constructive participation, to access the documentation produced, making it impossible to use their processes for other development teams.

Carioca [5] proposes a process of software testing assigned to the characteristics and specificities of Ginga, which focuses not only on the maintenance of product quality, but also on the compliance, specification and validation of a given configuration middleware. The process is divided into three macros activities: (i) planning; (ii) specification; and (iii) execution and analysis. Interesting point common to our proposal is the similarity in the activities used in the process and the execution environment, although they have different implementations. The main aim of the paper is to address the verification and validation process, and perform unit testing and integration, and system testing, used as reference implementation for the Ginga, and evaluation was carried out through simulation tool. But the proposed work addresses system testing, also using the Ginga platform as execution environment, but assessment was performed in real products, with brands/models available.

Other research [6] [7] [8] [9], focuses on the implementation of software testing, using systematic testing usability testing, prototyping, unit testing, integration testing, performance testing, usability testing, infrastructure testing and compliance testing. Thus, none of the studies is a systematic approach that they can be repeated and evaluated in comparison with the proposal of this work. In addition, none of these works used market products for the implementation of their tests, only software emulating receiving terminals.

3   Software Testing

The society we live in is completely dependent on technology. From simple household appliances such as televisions, refrigerators or telephones, to means of transportation (eg., cars and planes), all of them contain software that is essential to its operation, and that if it can fails can have devastating consequences, both in terms of convenience and financial impact. The complexity of software requires that it possesses a high level of quality. Then, enter software testing, which is one of the main mechanisms to reduce the occurrence of problems and ensure the quality of the software produced.

Software testing is one of the main activities to improve and maintain the quality of a product under development. Its main purpose is to reveal the presence of errors in software systems as early as possible in the development cycle in order to minimize the cost of repairing these systems. According to Delamaro [1], the software testing activities seek to ensure that the product complies with the specifications. Have Bridges, [10] complements this information citing that the testing activities may account for a considerable share of the costs of a project, however he realizes that the vast majority of companies do not practice it, due to lack of qualified professionals to apply tests in the development process.

Pressman [11] classifies the tests as:

- Unit Testing: focuses on the effort to verify the smallest software unit. Its main objective is to find execution failure on a small part of the running system.
- Integration test: is a technique that detects errors associated with interfaces. Your goal is to ensure that the modules tested in the unit level, work when integrated.
- Validation test: the two possible validation test outputs are: compliance with the specifications of the outcome or deviation from the specifications by creating a defficiency list.
- System Test: It includes a set of tests whose primary purpose is to put in evidence the system. The system test can include recovery testing, security, stress and performance.
- Recovery test: is the test that forces the system to fail in many ways and verifies that the recovery has been properly executed.
- Security Testing: verifies that all built-in protection mechanisms in the system are in fact protecting unauthorized access to the system, etc. attacks
- Stress test: is performed to verify system behavior when it requires the same amount, frequency or data volume.
- Performance Testing: is used to test the performance of the software, considering the software and its integration. It is often combined with the stress test.

3.1   Software Test Procedure

A test procedure can be seen as a methodology for revealing defects in software and to establish if it reaches a certain level of quality. A software testing process consists of activities that aim to run a program in order to reveal its faults and assess their quality. [11] Thus, the test process is a vital component in a quality process.

The testing process includes a structuring phased, activities, artifacts, roles and responsibilities seeking the standardization of work, management and monitoring of test projects. The IEEE 829 [2] standard defines a set of documents (artifacts) for software testing activities, organized in three stages: (i) Test Preparation; (ii) Implementation of the Test and (iii) Test Record (Figure 1).

The activities are delegated to persons with special ability to execute them. There is no consensus in the literature on the possible roles in the testing process. However, the roles and responsibilities commonly found in [12] and [13] are: (i) Project Manager, the person who manages and represents the team of developers; (ii) Test Manager, the person who deals with all matters related to software testing; (iii) Test Engineer is primarily responsible for specifying and designing test cases; (iv) Tester, the person responsible for implementing, configuring and running the tests and therefore recording the results obtained; (v) Configuration Manager, the person who arranges the elements as a whole.

The documents to be defined, covering the planning, specification and execution of tests, stand out [2]:

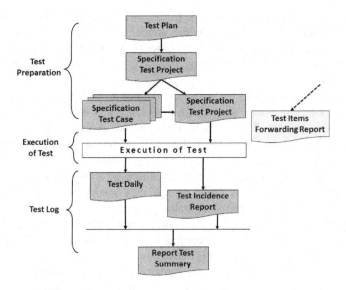

Fig. 1. IEEE 829 Standard for Software Test Documentation.

- Test Plan: Provides planning for test execution, including the scope, approach, resources and schedule of test activities. Identifies the items and features to be tested, the tasks to be performed and the risks associated with the testing activity.
- Test Project: refinement of the approach found in the Test Plan and identifies cases and test procedures (technical requirements of the testing process, based on the technology used in its implementation), if any, and presents the criteria for approval.
- Test Case: specifications that will be implemented, including input data, expected results, actions and conditions for the test run.
- Test statement: specifies the sequence of steps for performing one or more test cases.
- Report / Test Summary: presents a summary of the results of the testing activities associated with one or more test design specifications and provides ratings based on these results.
- Executing Test report: identifies the features implemented successfully and that failed or even runtime errors.

4 Test Methodology Proposal

The approach proposed in this paper aims to provide an assessment of the process of software testing development for products that implement the middleware Ginga. Based on this goal, you can set documents to: test plan, test design, test cases and test assertions to compose the set of documents necessary to evaluate the quality of the platform, using, specifically, system testing, as you can't have access to the source code of the products. In addition, there are documents, consisting of partial and general reports, formalizing the implementation of the adopted process.

The modeling procedure is based on [2]. The paper is composed of planning, specification and implementation analysis, which are defined and arranged to allow the test to be efficient and effective. To model this process, we used the EPF (Eclipse Process Framework), a tool for process modeling, aiming at the definition, customization and publication [14].

As presented in Figure 2, the approach defines a number of key activities to achieve good levels of quality in software products and is developed within the context of the testing process. These activities were based on phases (or levels of testing) of a traditional test process, with the inclusion of the return flow to the activities developed for a pretended refinement. Each activity is defined mainly as composed of tasks to be performed by their respective guardians, who take artifacts as documents necessary for their enforcement. These persons may accumulate roles during the development of the project as it is defined in the planning activity.

It is noteworthy that the process is completely adaptable, where the existing tasks in each activity can be carried out, according to the need and the real design environment. Thus there may be the use of documents made available by other projects, there are tasks in some activities that will not run. However, the reviewing task present in each activity in a mandatory manner, there is confirmation of truthfulness and cover all generated or available documentation.

Therefore, it is emphasized that the process is performed incrementally, interactions occurring during the development of the test project. The approach provides guidelines for the implementation of test strategies in the process. The following will detail each step in the proposed process.

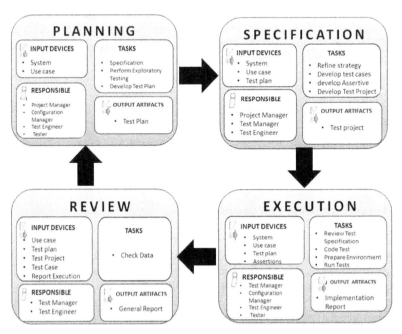

Fig. 2. Process overview

4.1   Planning

Planning is an entity composed of three tasks that are performed sequentially: (1) to study the system specification, (2) perform exploratory testing and (3) develop a test plan.

The task of studying the system specification aims to understand the functioning and middleware rules as an integrated system that will be tested, according to the use cases, equipment (TVs and converters) and the features available for testing. Input devices formed by the system.

The task to perform exploratory testing is to use the equipment and applications involved in the test, so as to know the developed features such as, navigation and objectives. Those responsible for this task choose what will be tested, when and how to test it, since it is performed individually. In addition, those responsible may vary some aspects during the implementation of the tests rather than repeat them in the same way continuously.

The development of the test plan is characterized by building a document that has a detailed modeling workflow executed during the process, and includes details such as: (i) the scope, (ii) the approach, (iii) the resources used and (iv) the schedule of activities. Those responsible must also define which tools are used to identify the test phases, build teamwork, and provide the test plan for the remaining steps of the process. Based on this information, the test plan document is prepared.

Finally, the planning activity requires the involvement of all actors (project manager, test manager, configuration manager, test engineer and the tester) that form the staff of the testing process proposed in this paper.

4.2   Specification

Specifying activities consists of four tasks also performed sequentially: (1) refine strategy, (2) prepare test cases, (3) develop assertive and (4) develop test project.

The refinement of the strategy aims to review the test plan prepared during the planning activity. For use assure the quality of the document. For the task to be performed requires the presence of a project manager, a test manager and test engineer. Input devices are formed by use cases and the system.

The preparation of test cases is a task used as a reference in coding the tests. However, they can be changed during the development, making it more appropriate to the behavior shown by the product during the performance of tasks. Use cases and the test plan are important input artifacts for the development of the task. The output artifacts of this task are the cases of specified tests.

Complementing the information of the use cases, this is the task of use information such as the expected inputs and outputs to validate an individual unit of functionality or behavior derived from the statements contained in the specification to be tested.

Finally, the test design is prepared. The test project document is part of the specification documents and contains the set of test cases and assertions, noting which test cases will be encoded and therefore executed.

4.3   Execution

In the activity implentation phase, the following tasks are present: reviewing the specifications, code testing, preparing the execution and the execution of test applications. In Figure 3 should be located at the end of the sentence.

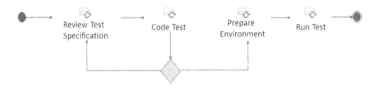

Fig. 3. Flowchart Execution of activity

Initially, the review of the test specifications must be performed to ensure the coverage of generated test cases, and thus validate the system and the quality of test applications. This task has the participation of the test manager and test engineer, analyzing the test plan, test cases and their respective assertions and the test project. Thus, the design specification is completed and proceeds to the coding task.

In the test code task, the tester generates new applications of test cases or perform improvements / fixes in applications of existing test cases according to the test project, the use cases and assertive. After that, the test applications are released by the tester to the third task, environment preparation, configuration manager that organizes the equipment, personnel and local applications to be implemented as defined in the planning.

When carrying out the tests, the applications defined in the test project document are implemented and an implementation report is produced. If the results are incompatible with the specifications, the problem should be referred to the responsible specifying activity or planning according to the analysis of the tester, so as to be solved.

4.4   Review

In the analysis of activity, the main objective is to build a general report, which will present relevant information of the activities performed during the process. Furthermore, the document will include information such as: (i) the number of test cases executed, (ii) the number of cases that successfully executed tests (iii) the number of test cases performed partially (presence of failure), and (iv) number of test cases that did not execute. These data are based on generated artifacts, for example, the execution report.

Since the constructed document will be published in order to assist in future projects, both test development team, as the external teams (of new TV manufacturer's teams). Therefore, it is necessary that we have a clear assessment, accurate, and consistent document before its publication, making sure that the information available is in accordance with the actual results of the evaluation.

5   Evaluation

To evaluate the proposed approach an evaluation with Ginga platform was performed. As a starting point, due to the time constraint, we used a test suite which was previously developed. However, this aspect has confirmed the possibility of using third-party documents to carry out some activities of the proposed process. Another important point was the utilization test environment similar to a production environment of a TV station. Such an environment consisted of: (1) four commercial receivers available on the market represented by four different labels; (2) audio and video files generated from recording live programs of national broadcasters; and (3) transmission infrastructure composed of signal multiplexer (responsible for the union of audio streams, video and data into a single transport stream), data carousel generator (responsible for entering data from applications on the TV signal) and a modulator (responsible for sending the transport stream through the air).

The process adopted was presented by the test manager to other team members, therefore, there was the possibility of them opinions so as to improve the process that would be used in addition to the knowledge of how would run the activities. Next section details the aspects related to Ginga-NCL tests.

5.1   Ginga-NCL

Ginga-NCL, created by PUC-Rio, was created in order to provide a presentation system for declarative applications written in NCL, which is a declarative XML-based language, whose main characteristics the possibility of specification with interactive features, timeline synchronization between media objects, adaptability, support for multiple devices and support live edition of nonlinear interactive programs.

A main component of Ginga-NCL is the interpretation machine declarative content (NCL formatter). Other important modules are the player (user agent) XHTML and presentation engine Lua, the latter responsible for the inter pretend of the Lua [15] scripts, Lua is a programming language based on light scripts, interpreted and easy to use.

The NCL declarative language is based on the NCM (Nested Context Model), which shows the relationship of the NCM model entities with NCL elements (Figure 4).

Given the structure of the elements presented above, during the course of the planning activity, set up using the test suite available for the project "Ginga-NCL Conformance Testing" of the PUC-RIO TeleMídia, composed of 549 test cases, divided for 17 elements (Area, Bind, BindParam, CasualConnector, Context, compoundCondition, connectorParam, Descriptor, ImportedDocumentBasei, importNCL, Link, linkParam, Media Port, Property, and simpleAction simpleCondition), where these are defined in ABNT NBR 15606-2 [17].

As the output device in the planning activity, a test plan was built. The document is detailed function and LIABILITY of each person on the team, test strategy used, the test environment required to run the tests, and the planned schedule for all iterations.

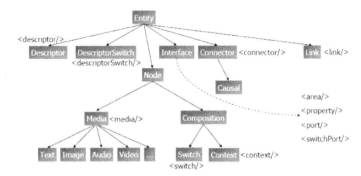

Fig. 4. Relationship of the NCM model entities with the elements of NCL [16].

In the test specification activity, the process adaptability was, not to specify the assertions document, whereas the test cases were classified as "simple", since they did not require user interaction, but only the observation of the same applications run. As test cases were built, it was decided to use them in the same existing model, carrying out a review in the document. Following the model of the proposed process, the artifact of the test project was drawn up specifying which test cases would be referred to the run activity, helping the tester to perform the activity.

When submitting the file to the other team members, the team Realized The Possibility expose the view as well, there Were improvements to be ADOPTED in the process, fouled the acquisition of knowledge to perform the activities. In the next section details the aspects related to Ginga-NCL tests.

5.2   Test Results

The implementation of all available testing applications had a total duration of 93 hours.

From the 549 test cases available and implemented for Ginga-NCL, there was a significant difference in results when compared to each TV set. It was found that 299 applications performed successfully in Model 1, 286 applications in Model 2, 79 applications in Model 3 and 278 applications in model 4 (Figure 5).

For full coverage of the test suite, four process iterations were executed, which were classified in alphabetical order of the suite of elements. These iterations were on the minimum time to complete the execution of the available applications.

In all the there were factors that contributed significantly in the development of the testing process, which can be highlighted: (1) implementation of a clear and objective way process and (2) the availability of test cases and application already completed for another project; (3) the amount of review tasks present at the beginning of each activity specified in the proposed software process. Since there were already test cases and ready applications, this phase contributed enough so that those responsible were directed in quantity level, quality, and coverage of the tests; and (4) performance variation of the TV sets with respect to all cases of testing performed during the whole process, which further reinforced the need for quality assessment mechanisms of this product available to consumers.

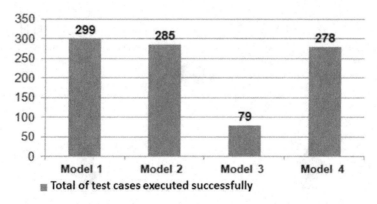

Fig. 5. Overall performance of television sets.

The activities could be managed and planned in a concise manner, although flaws in the process have been identified, such as the preparation of the test infrastructure. In other words, it was possible to implement the process, but as lessons learned existed a need for a test environment and to support the existence of a document that has traceability between the test cases and the evaluation results.

Element	Total Test	NOT RUN				RUN FAILED				SUCCESSFULLY EXECUTED			
		Model 1	Model 2	Model 3	Model 4	Model 1	Model 2	Model 3	Model 4	Model 1	Model 2	Model 3	Model 4
Area	20	4	4	20	4	3	3	0	3	13	13	0	13
Bind	27	22	2	27	2	3	3	0	3	22	22	0	22
BindParam	2	0	0	2	0	0	0	0	0	2	2	0	2
CausalConnector	3	0	0	3	0	0	0	0	0	3	3	0	3
CompoundCondition	6	0	0	6	0	3	3	0	3	3	3	0	3
ConnectorParam	2	0	0	1	0	1	1	0	1	1	1	0	1
Context	8	0	0	8	0	0	0	0	0	8	8	0	8
Descriptor	40	9	30	22	18	8	0	2	1	23	10	16	21
ImportedDocumentBase	1	0	1	1	0	0	0	0	0	1	0	0	1
ImportNCL	1	0	1	1	0	0	0	0	0	1	0	0	1
Link	6	0	6	6	0	1	0	0	1	5	0	0	5
LinkParam	2	0	2	2	0	0	0	0	0	2	0	0	2
Media	71	37	44	54	39	8	7	0	10	26	20	17	21
Port	20	6	7	18	8	0	0	0	0	14	13	2	12
Property	289	90	86	215	106	67	55	30	63	132	148	44	120
SimpleAction	27	0	0	27	0	7	7	0	7	20	20	0	20
SimpleCondition	24	0	0	24	0	1	1	0	1	23	23	0	23

Fig. 6. Detailed results of the execution test

In Figure 6 present data that expose the results by element for each TV model, which provides a quality the detailed view and quantity of test cases executed during the testing process developed and describe the large number of test cases and the variation in performance on each device.

Figure 7 shows the instance of the software testing process adopted and displays all the documents used as a precondition for the realization of activities and hence the artifacts created during the execution of it, thus including their respective officers and tasks who were present in the evaluation.

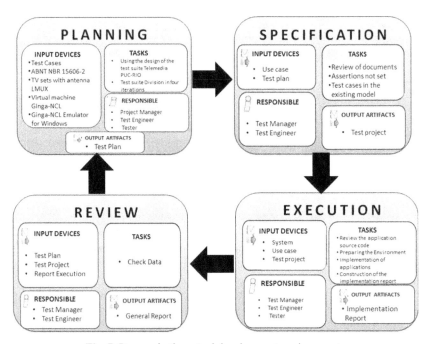

Fig. 7. Process in the actual development environment

6   Conclusion

This study present a software testing process that addresses a plan of basic tasks of tests to be performed, helping supervised development of the quality of the elements of middleware Ginga-NCL SBTVD. One of the goals achieved with this work, was the construction of the artifacts as a way to test the generated results. In addition, the test results can also be used to evaluate the conformity of the implementation of the middleware Ginga-NCL elements according to their specification.

Since the project is based on a test suite already defined by another project, much attention and understanding with respect to the information that was available in the suite of documentation was required. However, it was found that the proposed process was appropriate to this situation, since it includes task analysis and review of the artifacts used in the activities.

Another important point to mention is that the process execution results, even with a limited scope to Ginga-NCL and use of television models purchased in late 2012, have helped to note that it is still necessary to better define the compliance criteria and quality that an implementation of the Ginga middleware should have to be released on the market. Otherwise, there is a great risk that existing devices on the market that will not offer the functionalities provided in the specifications platform of Ginga.

This work opens up new opportunities in software testing area related to Digital TV and can have as future work: (1) inclusion of newer models receiving terminals (TV sets); (2) generation of new case studies, using elements and products;

(3) improvement of the specifications of test cases and assertive; (4) construction of new test cases, assertive and applications; and (5) expand the test coverage level, including Ginga middleware elements.

References

1. Delamaro, E., Maldonado, J.C., Jino, M.: Introdução ao teste de software. Elsevier, Rio de Janeiro (2007)
2. IEEE 829 - 1998. IEEE Std. 829. Standard for Software Test Documentation (1998)
3. NISOFT. Disponível em: http://www.unisoft.com/. Acesso em: 30 de ago. 2014
4. MHP-CONFIDENCE. Disponível em: http://www.irt.de/mhp-confidence/. Acesso em: 30 de ago. 2014
5. Caroca, C.R.: Um Processo de Verificação e Validação para o Middleware Ginga. João Pessoa. Dissertação de Mestrado UFPB (2010)
6. Cruz, V.M., Moren, M.F., Soares, L.F.G.: Ginga-NCL: Implementação de Referência para Dispositivos Portáteis, pp. 67–74. ACM, New York (2008)
7. Flores, L.V., Faust R., Pimenta M.S.: Definindo uma Proposta para Avaliações de Usabilidade de Aplicações para o Sistema Brasileiro de TV Digital. In: IHC 2008 – VIII Simpósio Sobre Fatores Humanos em Sistemas Computacionais. Porto Alegre, 21–24 out. 2008
8. Marques Neto, M.C., Santos, C.A.S.: StoryToCode: Um Modelo baseado em componentes para especificação de aplicações de TV Digital e Interativa convergentes. In: XV WebMedia, 2009, Fortaleza. SBC, 2009, vol. 1, pp. 59–66 (2009)
9. Araújo, E.C., et al.: Nested Context Language 3.0 Parte 14 - Suíte de Testes de Conformidade para o Ginga-NCL. Monografia da Pontifícia Universidade Católica do Rio De Janeiro - Departamento de Informática (2011)
10. Pontes, M.B.: Introdução a testes de software, Engenharia de Software Magazine, ano 1 (2009)
11. Pressman, R.S.: Engenharia de Software. Makron books, São Paulo (1995)
12. Burnstein, I.: Practical software testing: a process-oriented approach. Springer, New York (2003)
13. Molinari, L.: Testes de software - Produzindo Sistemas Melhores e mais confiáveis, 2a, São Paulo: Ed. Érica (2003)
14. EPF. 2014. Eclipse Process Framework (2014). Disponível em: www.eclipse.org/epf/. Acesso em: 30 ago. 2014
15. ABNT NBR 15606-5. Televisão digital terrestre - Codificação de dados e especificações de transmissão para radiodifusão digital Parte 5: Ginga-NCL para receptores portáteis – Linguagem de aplicação XML para codificação de aplicações (2008)
16. Soares, L.F.S., Rodrigues, R.F.: Nested Context Model 3.0 Part 1 — NCM Core. Monografias em Ciência da Computação do Departamento de Informática, PUC-Rio (2005)
17. ABNT NBR 15606-2. Televisão digital terrestre – Codificação de dados e especificações de transmissão para radiodifusão digital Parte 2: Ginga-NCL para receptores fixos e móveis – Linguagem de aplicação XML para codificação de aplicações (2008)

Evaluation of the Waiting Time Tolerance of User Authentication in Custom Applications of IDTV

Luis Nícolas de Amorim Trigo[1(✉)] and Carlos André Guimarães Ferraz[2(✉)]

[1] Campus Petrolina, Federal Institute of Education,
Science and Technology of Sertao Pernambucano, Petrolina, Pernambuco 56314-520, Brazil
nicolas.trigo@ifsertao-pe.edu.br
[2] Informatics Center, Federal University of Pernambuco, Recife,
Pernambuco 50740-540, Brazil
cagf@cin.ufpe.br

Abstract. This study aims to present an analysis of the tolerance of the wait time for DTV viewers. To achieve this goal it is necessary to gather information on authentication and tolerance, evaluation criteria, develop a scenario of Digital TV environment in authentication process, simulating the proposed scenario and assess information generated by the implementation of the prototype. After the evaluation, if realized tolerance variations in the authentication of many viewers for a IDTV environment. The results of this study provide information that can be taken as a reference for studies on runtime, covering the performance level of the product, leading to a substantial quality that is efficiency.

Keywords: Authentication methods · IDTV · Wait time

1   Introduction

Currently, viewers take the passive attitude to TV sets. Since the appearance of Interactive Digital Television (IDTV), viewers began to interact with the TV programming. This interaction takes place through applications that provide services such as the customization [1] [13].

This paper reports on the viewer's tolerance expect the completion of authentication in IDTV.

The goal of this work is the analysis of the tolerance of the waiting time for IDTV viewers. Therefore, it is necessary to gather information about authentication and about tolerance, set evaluation criteria, provides an overview of the authentication process in IDTV environment, simulating the proposed scenario and evaluate the information collected for the prototype's implementation.

This work is divided into five sections. In Section 2, the literature review will be addressed, this relation to authentication methods and safety criteria. Section 3 will describe the methodology adopted. Section 4 will show the results collected from analysis of the experiments through the methodology adopted. Section 5 will be exposed to conclusion and future work.

© Springer International Publishing Switzerland 2015
M.J. Abásolo and R. Kulesza (Eds.): jAUTI 2014, CCIS 389, pp. 74–82, 2015.
DOI: 10.1007/978-3-319-22656-9_6

2   Literature Review

This section presents an approach to authentication method and tolerance.

2.1   Authentication Method

The relationship of a person whom she says is can be answered by two actions: identification and authentication (Thian cited in [8]).

The word identification is defined as an act or effect of identifying or identify. Identify is to prove or recognize someone's identity. It is also becoming identical [12]. The same term in latin "*identicus*", means the same thing. Therefore, the identification corresponds determining the identity of a person initially unknown (Thian cited in [8]).

Already the word authentication, as [12], is defined as an act or effect of authenticating, this verb meaning "to declare authentic" (latim: *authenticus*), which is true. Also is to validate a particular identification, ie legitimize the person who tells you who it is or cancel such an action (Thian cited in [8]).

Some authentication methods are detailed and exemplified as:

- Fingerprint, this method uses the folds of skin found in the fingers and toes [2] [9] [10];
- Palm print, this method uses the format and palm skin folds [2];
- Facial Recognition, this method uses face geometric features, such as the distances and angles between eyes, eyebrows, nose, lips, and approaches based on appearance through facial expressions [2] [6] [10];
- Voice Recognition, this method uses physical characteristics of voice, considered unique to each individual, extracted for there to carry out the spectral analysis. [2] [6];
- Sole of the foot, this method uses extracted from standing features in a sensor mat, getting parts of the feet and the intensity of their pressure [11];
- Username and password, this method is very common in web applications and, through a pair of information, consists of an identification name and password (known character set only by the authenticated user), through a form, where together make up a unique ID [4] [5];
- Authentication matrix, this method is very common in the banking system. By means of a table consisting of a set of two numbers where the first number is an identification code and the second number is the password related to code [14];
- RFID (Radio-Frequency Identification), this method is very common with ATM cards and mobile phones. The RFID tag is a small object that contains silicon microchip and an antenna system that allows respond to radio signals from the RFID reader, which is why a transmitting base emission of radio signals to get the information answered by RFID tags [3] [4];

2.2   Tolerance

The word tolerance (latin: *tolerantia, tolero*) means support a weight or strength to endure something. This is a social or individual attitude that recognizes the right of others to have different opinions, and allows disseminate and express publicly or privately [7].

Thomas Aquinas said that tolerance is the same as patience, which is the good mood or love making people bearing the bad or unpleasant things. Over the centuries, many people spoke of religious, ecclesiastical or theological tolerance. Currently, also tolerates patiently at points that are not essential to a particular doctrine even if it is at the expense of it, but for a better social life. In medicine, the word tolerance is used to mean the ability of the organism to withstand the action of a drug, a chemical or physical agent. Thus, different species tolerant microorganisms in different ways: some get sick and die; nothing happens other [7].

With tolerance, people tend to be very complacent with misconduct for himself, and ruthless with others: the time required to change is insufficient. Change the way and act in a completely opposite way is a task that requires effort and can last long. For others it is required that all occur at once, forgetting that things have their natural rhythm. For example, a bean takes to germinate, grow, bloom, giving the pod, and people have attitudes of children, leaving the beans planted and where, the next day, are disappointed by the plant did not grow [7].

3   Methodology

This section will describe the evaluation criteria and the structuring of data collection of experiments on the analysis of the wait time tolerance viewer authentication scenario in IDTV.

3.1   Evaluation Criteria

The evaluation criteria used in this study corresponds to the waiting time tolerance. This criterion measures the time in seconds that the viewer waits for your authentication in IDTV.

3.2   Technical Information

A scenario, like a living room containing a sofa, chairs and a TV, was prepared for the experiment. It was not adopted a specific authentication method for this experiment. Authentication of respondents happen somehow through resources provided to the viewer during the experiment. Through this experiment it was possible to survey the time when a person bears wait until authenticated.

After identifying the authentication methods, the use cases for these methods have been produced will be used by the viewer of IDTV. Based on these use cases, generalized use case was proposed, covering the basic steps required for all authentication methods raised.

The steps of the use case generalized were detailed as follows:

- Viewer turn on the TV.
- Appears on the TV screen information to the viewer authentication procedure.
- The viewer enable identification data input device to initiate authentication.
- The TV's authentication system captures the viewer's data to perform the search in the registered user's database.
- The TV's authentication system identifies the viewer as a registered user allowing access to services available in IDTV.

From this generalized use case, a prototype was developed using XHTML and CSS technologies. This prototype was running on a computer connected to a TV via HDMI cable, simulating the real scenario necessary to capture the time a person waits to be identified by authentication system of IDTV.

The experiment conducted in this prototype worked in an environment similar to a living room. During the experiment, two people were present in this room: a viewer and an observer. The viewer sitting in a chair in front of the TV that will run the experiment. The observer monitored all experimental activities carried out by the viewer. He also had all steps to be performed by the viewer, except the outcome of the experiment. During the experiment, the observer monitored the viewer and wrote down information representing a anxiety reaction waiting for the authentication is completed. This information corresponds to the time (seconds) between the start of the execution of the experiment and the viewer's anxiety reaction.

The TV, through a computer connected by HDMI cable, run the authentication system prototype. The viewer sitting in the chair in front of the TV received the observer's instructions experiment. Then the observer reported that the viewer could start the experiment by pressing the on-screen icon displayed using the input device. This activity indicated the act of turning on the TV (Figure 1).

Turn on the TV

Fig. 1. TV screen showing icon mimicking the function of turning on the TV.

After pressing the icon, the instructions for viewer's authentication appeared on the TV screen. These instructions tell the viewer that it should use the input device by pressing on the image to start authentication. This image is formed by two people, one male and the other female. The observer asked for the viewer to read the instructions and communicating when he would be ready to start the experiment (Figure 2).

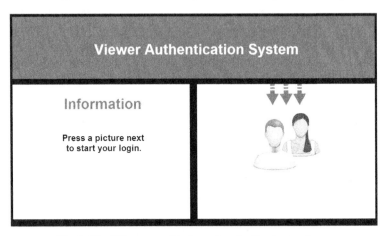

Fig. 2. The TV screen with the authentication instructions.

After the viewer to press the icon to start authentication, observers began to monitor the viewer performing the activity, connecting the timer and waiting for a reaction of anxiety. These reactions may be, for example, making any inquiry or look towards the viewer. This observer paralyzed the stopwatch to see one of these reactions and explaining the purpose of the experiment, recording the time that the viewer waiting for authentication is completed. Figure 3 shows a screen displayed on the TV while the viewer waits to be identified by authentication system of IDTV.

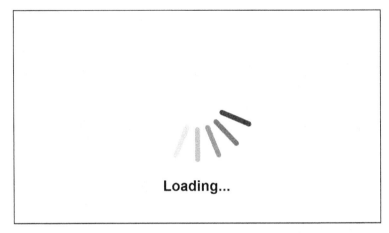

Fig. 3. The TV screen showing the viewer that the search in the registered user database is in progress.

3.3   Viewers

Thirteen people were asked to perform the experiment cited above. These people are men and women, aged 5 to 79 years, and are distributed in the following categories: elementary school, middle school, high school and graduate school.

Among all respondents, children and the elderly were the people most concerned observer as to the understanding of the experiment. The observer explained in detail the experiment, showing examples of similar procedures in other situations. For children, it was an example of user authentication online games and Internet. As for the elderly, in addition to the same examples presented for children, was presented an viewer's authentication example in the banking system, considered a common environment for people in this age group.

4   Results

In this section we describe the results of the data collected on the tolerance of the wait time by performing the viewer authentication experiments in IDTV.

Figure 4 shows that male viewers are less tolerant than female viewers.

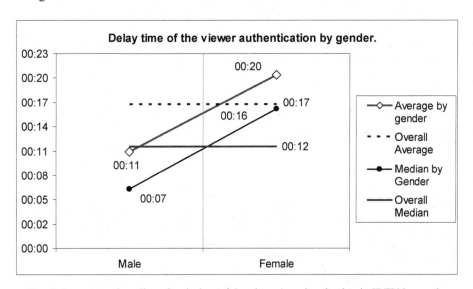

Fig. 4. Average and median of wait time of the viewer's authentication in IDTV by gender

Figure 5 shows a smaller degree of wait time tolerance in children and elderly, that is, among viewers between 0 and 20 years and 65 years to 86 years. Viewers between 21 and 65 years are more patients during their authentication.

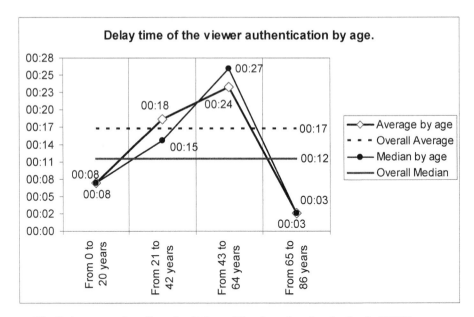

Fig. 5. Average and median of wait time of the viewer's authentication in IDTV by age.

Figure 6 shows that the wait time tolerance of viewer's authentication becomes longer when it has a higher level of education.

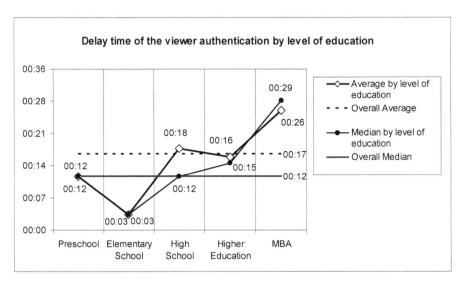

Fig. 6. Average and median of wait time of the viewer's authentication in IDTV by level of education.

After the completion of the experiment, viewers were informed that the objective was to raise the time they endured wait until your login in IDTV be completed. Then the observer wondered if they wanted to make a statement. The main statements were:

- *"I was waiting for something to happen and nothing happened. I wanted to ask for the observer would happen when the authentication, but did not want to move me not to be a problem with my authentication."*
- *"I thought it was some information appears on the screen, I was expecting something to happen, thinking it was anyway."*

Viewers comb their hair, stand still in front of the TV, watching the input device to start the authentication of the viewer, with the curiosity to know how they would be identified.

Thus, it was observed that some people have less tolerance than others. Figures 4, 5 and 6, children and the elderly are less tolerant. It is noticed that children are more active than people of other ages and do not end up waiting your login in IDTV when it begins to take longer than normal. The elderly, for not having lived with this type of technology, become more insecure, leading to be less tolerant. The history of mankind reports that women are more tolerant than men. People with access to information and higher education levels tend to be more tolerant.

In [15] shows that children have less tolerance while performing the activities of art classes, showing that this age group may be more hyperactive.

Already [16] reports that, in the professional field, women have physical attributes as kindness and tolerance and can relate that it is not only professional attributes, but they are part of women's routine.

In [17], in a scenario in the case of the subject homosexuality, older people are less tolerant than younger age groups, something similar to experimental reality of this work, because it is something out of the reality of day-to-day these people.

5   Conclusion

This study aimed to demonstrate the wait time tolerance for viewer's authentication in IDTV. For this, the concepts of authentication methods and tolerance were raised to be understood. A generalized use case of authentication methods applied in IDTV was developed to propose an experiment, getting results on tolerance considering gender, age and education level.

After analyzing the data collected from the experiment, it was identified that women are more tolerant than men, children and the elderly are less tolerant and the higher the level of a person's education, the more tolerant it tends to become.

These results presented information that can serve as reference for studies on runtime, encompassing product performance level, leading to the concept of efficiency. Also presents a scenario involving more proper authentication depending on the population studied.

For future work, study and viewers authentication tolerance experiments in other scenarios might be interesting, proposing to develop a set of information that will serve as a reference for studies in this area.

References

1. Blanco-Fernández, Y., et al.: TripFromTV+: Targeting personalized tourism to Interactive Digital TV viewers by social networking and semantic reasoning. IEEE Transactions on Consumer Electronics **57**(2), 953–961 (2011)
2. Corcoran, P., et al.: Biometric Access Control for Digital Media Streams in Home Networks. IEEE Transactions Consumer Electronics **53**(3), 917–925 (2007)
3. Jabbar, H., Jeong, T., Hwang, J., Park, G.: Viewer Identification and Authentication in IPTV using RFID Technique. IEEE Transactions on Consumer Electronics **54**(1) (2008)
4. Kim, S.-C., Yeo, S.-S., Kim, S.K.: A hybrid user authentication protocol for mobile IPTV service. Multimed. Tools Appl. **65**, 283–296 (2013). doi:10.1007/s11042-011-0810-5. Springer Science+Business Media: LLC, 2011
5. Kosch, H., Hölbling, G.: Application of recommendation methods for TV programs. In: IEEE, pp. 1–4 (2011)
6. Krevatin, I.: Biometric recognition in telecom environment. In: 14th International Conference on Intelligence in Next Generation Networks (ICIN), pp. 1–6 (2010)
7. Lacaz-Ruiz, R., de Oliveira, A.P., Scholtz, V., Anzai, N.H.: O Limite e a Tolerância. Disponível em: http://www.hottopos.com.br/vidlib2/o_limite_e_a_toler%C3%A2ncia.htm. Acessado em 4 jul 2014
8. Magalhães, P.S., dos Santos, H.D.: Biometria e autenticação, pp. 1–17 (2003). Disponível em: http://repositorium.sdum.uminho.pt/handle/1822/2184. Acessado em 30 set 2013
9. Mazi, R.C., Dal Pino Júnior, A.: Identificação Biométrica através da Impressão Digital usando Redes Neurais Artificiais. Anais do XIV ENCITA 2008, ITA, pp. 19–22 (2009)
10. Mlakar, T., Zaletelj, J., Tasic, J.F.: Viewer authentication for personalized iTV services. In: Eight International Workshop on Image Analysis for Multimedia Interactive Services (WIAMIS 2007), pp. 1–4 (2007)
11. Nose, S., Shimono, M., Nishiyama, M., et al.: Personal Identification based on Sole Pressure Distribution using a Hetero-core Optical Fiber Sensor Network for Personal Web Services. IEEE Computer Society. Congress on Services – I, 1–8 (2009)
12. Priberam: Dicionário Priberam da Língua Portuguesa (2013). Disponível em: http://www.priberam.pt/dlpo/. Acessado em 2 out 2013
13. Song, S., Moustafa, H., Afifi, H.: A survey on personalized TV and NGN services through context-awareness. ACM Computing Surveys (CSUR) **44**(1), 4 (2012)
14. Takamizawa, H., Tanaka, N.: User authentication method using topographical information of Google maps. In: International Conference in Green and Ubiquitous Technology, pp. 11–14. IEEE (2012)
15. Kishimoto, T.M.: Salas de aula de escolas infantis: Domínio da fila, tempo de espera e falta de autonomia da criança. Faculdade de Educação – USP. São Paulo. Nuances, vol. 5, número 5 (1999). Disponível em http://revista.fct.unesp.br/index.php/Nuances/article/viewArticle/90. Acessado em 29 ago 2014
16. Costa, T.B.: Gênero e Trabalho na 'Cidade do Aço'. Anais do I Simpósio sobre Estudos de Gênero e Políticas Públicas. Universidade Estadual de Londrina (2010). Disponível em http://www.uel.br/eventos/gpp/pages/arquivos/5.TaniaBassi.pdf. Acessado em 25 ago 2014
17. Walter, M.I.M.T.: A dualidade na inserção política, social e familiar do idoso: estudo comparado dos casos de Brasil, Espanha e Estados Unidos. Opinião Pública, vol 16, número 1. Campinas (2010). Disponível em http://dx.doi.org/10.1590/S010462762010000100008. Acessado em 30 ago 2014

Training to Improve the Performance of Usability Experts Involved in Developing Heuristic Evaluations for IDTV Applications

Delmys Pozo Zulueta[1(✉)], Adisleydis Rodríguez Alvarez[1], Yanet Brito Riverol[1],
Yeniset León Perdomo[2], Ailyn Febles Estrada[2], and Yusleydi Fernández del Monte[2]

[1] National Quality Center of Software, Calisoft, Havana, Cuba
delmysp@gmail.com, {aralvarez,ybrito}@uci.cu
[2] University of Informatics Sciences, UCI, Havana, Cuba
{yleonp,ailyn,ydelmonte}@uci.cu

Abstract. The Interactive Digital TV (IDTV) has the potential to provide motivation and dedication, also be an effective mean to promote learning in different surroundings [1]. The software´s products for IDTV should be more usable and more interactive, because they are intended for a public more diverse and to users less expert in the handling of information-technology systems.

Regardless of the methodology that is used to unroll these applications, usability is a topic that in the IDTV it is considered an indispensable attribute of quality.

This work shows up a strategy to accomplish heuristic evaluations in applications for the IDTV. In addition the paper presents a training process to manage usability knowledge in applications for the IDTV, taking into account the usability expert role as the most important one in the evaluation of this kind of applications.

Keywords: Usability · IDTV · Knowledge management

1 Introduction

The result of the evolution of television as the source of information has redounded in possessing today a Television of bigger quality, acquaintance for interactive Digital TV (IDTV). This technological jump has made possible that the users of this service become active. In informatics terms a program of IDTV is specific software that offers the users (televiewers) determined functionalities. The recent suchlike appearing of applications that as much has provision for specific characteristics functional like no functional reveal new problems in this area of the knowledge that they have not been approached like the developmental methodologies of these applications, the high-quality attributes that they should keep and the techniques to try them, between other ones. One of the problems that they accent is the need to achieve that the design of these new products of software keeps with elementary requirements that guarantee that they use themselves of correct way, what has associated with the attribute of

M.J. Abásolo and R. Kulesza (Eds.): jAUTI 2014, CCIS 389, pp. 83–102, 2015.
DOI: 10.1007/978-3-319-22656-9_7

quality defined as Usability. In this article we talk about some good practices to have in account when evaluating the usability in the applications unrolled for the IDTV. One of the problems that they accent is the need to achieve that the design of these new products of software keeps with elementary requirements that guarantee that they use themselves of correct way, what has associated with the attribute of quality defined as Usability.

At the present time, the focus of development of software for the IDTV is a theme under consideration, that not yet it is completely defined and for little-tried. Some works discuss the use of expeditious developmental methodologies of these applications but its advantages have not been properly proven in practice.

In Cuba because of the gradual introduction of the IDTV, it becomes necessary to establish bases to achieve that the developed applications have the usability required for the fulfillment of their objective: Interactivity. In terms of the changes that have implementing in Cuba relating to IDTV, was created the Software Evaluation Department (DEPS) that belong to Calisoft, a Usability group in Applications for the IDTV (GU IDTV), since this center is destined to evaluate the quality of the products that are unrolled in the country.

In the DEPS they evaluate all attributes of quality defined by the rules and international standards, in particular Usability. With the purpose of fulfilling the mission related with the production of applications for the IDTV with quality, the GU IDTV aims at creating and to design instruments and necessary processes to measure the usability in applications for the IDTV. As a result of years of work and investigation was designed a "Strategy to accomplish heuristic evaluations in applications for the IDTV".

The usability evaluation of a software system is one of the most important within the user-centered design stages, as it allows the usability characteristics of a system and insofar as the attributes, paradigms and usability principles that are implemented in it.

That is why the usability evaluation methods have become an interesting source of study for the usability researchers, application characteristics, the variety of methods and the results they deliver.

There are different types of usability evaluation methods, each with its own characteristics, which can be developed on different representations of the system, whether paper prototypes, software prototypes, finished systems and so on. These methods allow to establish communication between the user and developers, as the latter discover the goals, perceptions, problems and questions from users. In addition, usability evaluation methods for validating design decisions, discovering the problems and successes associated with the system, marking the differences and common thoughts, respectively, between developers and users.

The usability evaluation methods can be classified into two groups:

Usability Inspection Methods: Inspections interface design using empirical methods.

Usability Testing Methods: Empirical evidence of interface design with representative users.

Usability inspection methods evaluation correspond to that of usability interface design using heuristics inspections. They are based on analysis rather than experience. They are made by usability experts, and rely on the tour and analysis system being evaluated, identifying errors and design problems.

Given the conditions and characteristics of DEPS and knowledge acquired by specialists working for years turned into trained experts to perform these assessments it is that they decide to use as main method of assessment heuristic evaluations.

Heuristic Evaluation: A group of evaluators inspect the interface design based on the recognized principles of usability.

Heuristic evaluation (HE) is a usability evaluation method in which a small group of testers, usability specialists generally systematically inspect the interface design of the system in question based on the principles of usability, also called heuristic principles or simply heuristics.

This method of evaluation of usability is the most popular methods of inspection, basically for its ease and speed of implementation. It can be performed at different stages of development of software, even very early, so that the availability of a complete version of the system is necessary. Although the method is simple, the problems are not necessarily easy to find, always depending on the amount and level of the evaluators.

After consulting different literature sources it was decided to adopt the concept for this research given by Jakob Nielsen on heuristic evaluation because it is the one that applies to this research, as it presents an approach to the expert evaluators, major players of this article.

Jakob Nielsen [2] defines the heuristic evaluation as "the common noun of a group of methods once expert reviewers that check or examine aspects related with the usability of a user interface were based on".

When was used the strategy in the execution of heuristic evaluations in applications for the IDTV unrolled in the UCI [3] [4] and in Cuba, became aware of the problem that this strategy just like other ones investigated they centered around guides to organize the process of evaluation of Usability, defining roles, activities, the directrix that should be evaluated, but they do not take into account the main link of the heuristic evaluations: The expert in usability. The same it is indispensable for success and the obtaining of reliable results in the evaluations of applications for the IDTV, taking into account their own competitions and knowledge. The list of the directrix to evaluate can be perfect but this will not produce reliable results if they do not do not count with better and more qualified in the theme (experts in usability).

The selected experts should count on the necessary knowledge to perform their role; that way they will be able to be objectives and efficient in the detection of the No conformities (NC) [5].

Some topical researches define the expert in usability as a new profession that happened with the vertiginous development of Internet.

The performance of any profession needs the knowledge of determined competences. As affirms Jessup, these can define themselves like the specific group of skillful actions and necessary qualities to develop a job Individual and assuming a professional role [6]. Judging the usability of a system before being delivered to the customer gives Objective information to improve it and to avoid problems. In order to carry this task it´s necessary to count with Specialists with a level of abilities and determined knowledge.

Because there is not specific formation that he teaches how to be an expert on usability, becomes necessary that the institutions that want to accomplish this type of evaluation center also your efforts in educating experts of usability and negotiating the knowledge of the same of "*way that the information that it takes can be obtained, to store it, to transfer it, and looking for a better way of organizing her in order that it is more accessible for those concerned in the theme and obtaining better results in your work*" [7] .

For it this article shows a summary of the stages defined in the Strategy to accomplish heuristic evaluations in applications for the IDTV and describe in him a process of training designed to negotiate the knowledge of the experts in usability, in the theme of usability in applications for the IDTV.

The article is divided into two parts; in the first place the strategy of evaluation is described and second stages, activities, roles and tasks that conform the process of training. He will finish this work highlighting a series of findings and the bibliography searched for investigation.

2   Development

2.1   Heuristic Evaluations in Applications for the IDTV

Previously it is mentioned than the GU IDTV developed a Strategy to accomplish heuristic evaluations in applications for the IDTV (Figure 1). Their objective is supplying a guideline or course of action, step by step, that it enables evaluating the usability of the applications for the intervening IDTV heuristic evaluations, specifying how to carry out the corresponding activities to the evaluation and orientating on the principles, rules, regulations and general provisions to have in account to develop these tests. They define the roles that participate and their responsibilities (Table 1) and show up a set of good practices based in the experience of some specialists of IDTV in the execution of the tests. Finally appear the classification of the No Conformities for type of evaluation of usability.

The roles Coordinator of Usability IDTV and Tester of Usability IDTV are the ones that accomplish the function of experts that it takes in the heuristic evaluations, in turn the Coordinator of usability IDTV would be the boss of the team of expert reviewers.

Next is indicated a set of good practices that they should take into account the roles defined previously at the time of executing the process of tests. These are based on the experience of the specialists in IDTV.

Table 1. Roles and responsibilities of the experts in usability defined in strategy

Role	Responsibilities
Leader of GU IDTV	He is in charge of distributing the work of equitable way. He should take into account the competitions of the Tester of Usability IDTV and Coordinator of Usability IDTV when assigning them to determined evaluation.
Coordinator of usability IDTV	He is in charge of guiding the process of heuristic evaluation.
Tester of usability IDTV	He is responsible for inspecting the application to verify the enforcement of the designing directrix of the applications for the IDTV.

Leader of GU IDTV

• Distributing the work of equitable way.
• Taking into account the competitions of the Testers of Usability IDTV and Coordinator of Usability IDTV to assign them to an evaluation.

Tester of Usability IDTV

• Having usability report and checklist before starting the evaluation.
• Counting on the Report of Usability and checklist before beginning the evaluation.
• Requesting the help to Coordinator of Usability IDTV whenever required or have any questions.
• Keeping all the times a good communication with the Coordinator of Usability.
• Facilitate to the Coordinator of Usability all the information that this requests in minimal time.
• Conciliate the NC Usability.
• Being patient and exhaustive during the test.

Coordinator of Usability IDTV

• Requesting in the Design Workshop the necessary information to begin the evaluation of usability.
• Keeping updated the Usability Report.
• Select and update the checklist that he will apply according to the characteristics of the artefact.
• Distribute Tester of usability IDTV the checklist and Usability Report.
• Conciliate with each IDTV NC detected.
• Provide to the Tester of Usability IDTV the all information that is requests as soon as possible.
• Register on the Redmine (or any other management tool nonconformities) final NC registered Usability Report.
• Verify the solution of the NC.
• Maintaining all the times a good communication with the Tester of usability IDTV.

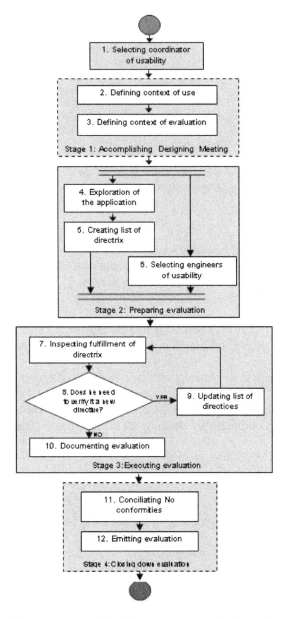

Fig. 1. Representation summarize of the "Strategy to accomplish heuristic evaluations in applications for the IDTV".

2.2   Stages of Strategy

Stage 1. Accomplishing designing reunion

The designing reunion is an encounter that is done between the team of development and reviewers of the different characteristics of quality. It is where the

Coordinator of Usability IDTV defines the context of use and of evaluation of the application.

Stage 2. Preparing evaluation

In this stage they sit host to accomplish the evaluation. The Coordinator of Usability IDTV accomplishes an exploration of the application. Then taking like base from characteristics the system, the service that he offers [8] and directrix, the Coordinator of Usability IDTV creates the list of directrix to evaluate that it applies to the system in point (Table 2).

Table 2. Interactive in the IDTV

Interactive services	Description
Information Services	They are the services that provide the user information of any kind (without being this once the programming that is emitted at that moment was related to). Some examples of these services can be meteorological information, cost-reducing or Stock-Exchange, traffic, etc.
Services associated to programming	These provide complementary information on the audiovisual contents that are Interactive in the IDTV they are emitting as of the present moment. Between these services Electronic Programation guide advanced (EPG), improved teletexts stand out.
Services of T-Commerce	They are those that allow the spectator acquiring products through your television set (for example, if in a program a critic acquires a book that the onlooker can buy it through Amazon).
Services of T-Administration	They allow the user accomplishing procedures through the TV, as requesting appointment in toilets, negotiating taxes, requesting forms to public administrations.
Services of T-Assistance	Supports are dependents through their radio receivers of TV (for instance remembering their schedules of the medications).
Services of Entertainment and Commercials	This category includes, on the one hand, services guided to the user's leisure and, for another one, services in order that companies catch this's attention. This category includes, on the one hand, services guided to the user's leisure and, for another one. They would enter the purchase of sporting events here also or movies in pay per view. In the second case we have like more obvious example the interactive orientated publicity to the user according to your interests.

The indicators that are selected to conform the list are structured so that they validate the heuristic ones defined by Nielsen and carried to the field of the IDTV by [9]:

• **Visibility:** In relation to aspects: How he shows up clearly, where the user meets or if the possible links to explore are identifiable.

• **Relation between the system and the real world:** In this aspect he tries to identify referent elements for him to if words, sentences and used concepts are familiar to the user, the sequence of activities obeys the thinking process of the users, the information is presented in simple, natural way and in order logical, and the used metaphors are easily understandable to the user.

• **Controlee and the user's freedom:** He tries to evaluate his elements such like, the ease to redo, to undo or to cancel options, the existence of clearly marked exits, the ease to give back the immediately previous point and the ease to give back the main menu from any place.

• **Consistence and standards:** Such evaluate aspects themselves like, if the application is consistent, the use of terms, symbols, controlees, graphics and menu in the whole application, if there is a coherent appearance, if there is consistency between the standard programs and the ones of ITV and if colors are consistent between both programs.

• **Prevention of errors:** He tries to evaluate his mechanisms that stock up to prevent errors themselves, evaluating aspects I eat: If there are messages that prevent possible errors, if possible foreseeing possible errors, or if the application does not induce to make mistakes.

• **Recognize more to remember:** In this aspect he tries to evaluate his capacity of using the application intuitively, asking aspects how if the relation between controlees and actions is obvious, if there are formats from the start and units of values indicated explicitly or if icons are recognizable.

• **Flexibility and efficiency of use:** The system allows to a status of expertise of the users, are guides for the newcomer users?

• **Esthetics and minimalistic design:** He tries to evaluate his aspect of visual design of the application identifying if the design is simple, intuitive, easy to learn and pleasant to use, the buttons and icons are well labeled, the use of the graphic controlees is obvious, is scroll when it is necessary and if there are the navigational ease and they are available always, if the content is well-classified and organized.

• **Help and documentation:** It is evaluated if there is some type of help or indication in the application, when there is help, this is specific and if help is accessible.

• **Help to recover from the errors:** He tries to evaluate the capacity of the application to resolve the found problems evaluating aspects as if error messages describe problems sufficiently, if they attend and they suggest mechanisms of recuperation and if they are written in constructive way without trying offending the user.

• **Navigation:** There is a hierarchic organization of the information from what's general to what's specific, the text length is appropriate to the size of the device and device of interaction; the titles are short and descriptive.

• **Physical limitations:** The screen is visible in different status of distance and several types of illumination, he separates her between the targets (e.g.: Icons) and its size is appropriate (size should be proportional to the distance).

• **Extraordinary user:** The use of the color is restricted appropriately (for users with visual problems), the use of the sound is restricted appropriately (for users with auditive problems).

Stage 3. Executing evaluation

Already in this stage the list of directrix that will evaluate themselves and that have been once the reviewers of usability were selected finds itself designed IDTV. The number of reviewers should be of three at least. The Reviewer of usability IDTV is who inspects the application to verify the fulfillment of the directrix selected previously by the Coordinator of Usability IDTV. If in the execution of judgment some Tester of Usability IDTV sees the need to incorporate any directive, can add it to the list and going on with the evaluation.

With the aim of getting the excellence in the service of heuristic evaluations it is necessary for the experts that intervene should have had competences and necessary knowledge to be able to perform their role and this has to be validated. Therefore; the members of the GU IDTV to be able to perform Tester's role of usability IDTV have to have spent a training period (a year) and to have participated like observer in the evaluations accomplished at that time. When he obtains that role to him periodic evaluations of their performance will come true. In order to choose the role of Coordinator of Usability IDTV for two years should perform in the appraising role of usability at the very least and obtaining satisfactory in all the evaluations that had been accomplished. Standing out is of value than the people that they obtain the Coordinating role of usability IDTV also they accomplish evaluations periodically.

As it is described, in this stage it is pretended that experts obtain experiences and that way keep on acquiring expertise, which is not enough, which is why to hold a continuous training based in a Knowledge Management System with the aim of allowing the GU's members IDTV the interaction with the information led to measure the usability in applications for the intervening IDTV becomes necessary heuristic evaluations.

Stage 4. Close evaluation

In this stage all reviewers put the No Conformities detected and in order they check in at an only report. A quantitative result of the evaluation also is broadcast. (Final Evaluation Report of Usability IDTV). This document is given to the developer of the product to assess the evidence of the evaluation. A quantitative evaluation result is also output. The sections and descriptions available to the Final Report are presented:

1. Introduction
   a) Objectives: Document the NC negotiated in the course of Evaluation of Usability.

2. Description of the Usability Evaluation.
   In the process of evaluation was used the supervisory method to achieve the objective of evaluation proposed and to measure the following attributes of usability:

Objective evaluation: *[The objective of the evaluation that was defined in the designing workshop is specified]*
Sub-characteristics of Usability to evaluate (ISO 25010): *[Are specified the sub-characteristic of usability that they measured].*
_____A esthetic user interface
_____Ability to be used
_____Capacity to recognize their suitability
_____Learning capacity
_____Protection against user errors
_____Capacity to recognize their suitability
_____Learning capacity
_____Protection against user errors

The evaluation was based on the fallowing context of use:

Access level: *[It defines what will be the network access device: Internal Network, National Network Internet].*

System type: *[Type of application is defined: Web Site, Desktop Application, Virtual Learning Environment, Multimedia, Game, etc.]*

Description of the end user: *[The user is described]*

System description: *[Brief description of the system]*

Main stages: *[Specified the functionalities more used in the system]*

Browser:

The testers used browsers and tools indicated below:

Principal browsers: *[The browser and the version used by the evaluator are specified].*

Auxiliary browsers: *[browsers and version used to test compatibility are specified].*

Tools: *[tools or support plugin used are specified].*

3. General Results Usability Assessment (the positive aspects of the evaluated product are described).

   a. Results. The assessment provided by the product is "X%" Usability, statistics for each sub-characteristics are:

Total of No Conformities		X NC	
Usability attribute	**% of Complete**	**Classification**	**Quantity**
Esthetics of the user interface	X %	Type 1	X NC
		Type 2	X NC
		Type 3	X NC
Capacity to be used	X %	Type 1	X NC
		Type 2	X NC
		Type 3	X NC
Learning capacity	X %	Type 1	X NC
		Type 2	X NC
		Type 3	X NC
Protection against user errors	X %	Type 1	X NC
		Type 2	X NC
		Type 3	X NC

In the following section are recorded the No Conformities detected and the improving actions that should be done. The improving actions are observations, explicit information and suggestions to help the detected deficiency.

4. Register of No Conformities

Description	Location	Importance Level	Classifica-tion	Improvement ac-tions
Artefact: Artefact name				
High-quality Attributes: *[Specified to than attribute of usability these NC belong.]*				
1				
2				

Legend:
Level of Importance: the importance of the NC is placed:

• Significant: NC affecting application performance.
• No Significant: NC not affects application performance.

Classification:
If the NC is significant you must select which type is significant.
If the NC is of the application is classified as:

• Interface error
• Compatibility
• Navigability
• User control
• Visibility
• Legibility
• Quality of content
• Language failure.

Improvement actions:
They provide observations, explicit information and suggestions to help the designer to improve the detected deficiency.

5. Annex: *[If is necessary]*

End of Final Evaluation Report of Usability IDTV

No Conformities are problems detected in a device according to the dissatisfaction with the final result of an objective assessment or not complying with a requirement. Then the classification to be given to the non-conformities identified during the evaluation process with the corresponding description is described (Table 3).

2.3   Process of Training to Negotiate Knowledge of Usability in Software's for the IDTV

Although the results obtained with the implementation of the strategy described were positive because we were able to improve the organization and quality of the evaluators work, it was found that the level of knowledge and training of the experts was not the same. It became necessary to define a process that establishing definitions, roles and stages contribute to the knowledge management of the DPSW experts.

Table 3. Classification of No Conformities

Classification	Description
Interface error	Problems that impact the interface affect the esthetics and visibility.
Compatibility	Problems that have an effect on the interface than not allow to visualization and correct use of the system in the equipments of visualization.
Navigability	Problems affecting the displacement or user navigation.
User control	Problems that affect on the control on behalf of the user of the relevant actions that he realizes.
Visibility	Problems that have an effect on what the user perceives on what happens.
Legibility	Problems that have an effect on the reading of the published content.
Quality of content	Problem affecting the importance and veracity of published content.
Language failure	Problem that have an effect on the importance and veracity of the published content.

Made out a process of training, consisting of a model to negotiate knowledge about the usability in applications for the IDTV. In the Figure 2 that the model consists of four stages to establish it appraises itself, shaped for activities and tasks that allow obtaining the objectives of every stage. Each task has required receipts and expenditures, that they can be generated documents or realized actions, among others. The way out of a task can represent the entry of another one, and that way always a cycle of training would come true.

The stages that observe themselves in the Figure 2 are: Planning and documentation, Acquisition of knowledge, Developer of the media of transmission of knowledge and Evaluation and monitoring of the system. In order to implement the stages that proposes the process a plan that works ensues iterative and increasingly. When defining the roles that would intervene in the process IDTV decided to hold it the roles already established in the GU, but added new responsibilities like sample themselves the Table 4.

2.4   Stage of the Knowledge Management System

Stage 1. Planning and Documentation

At this stage it is created an infrastructure where the work plan that generates a schedule is done, considering how each task is fulfilled, the time and responsible for it.

Deficient knowledge is diagnosed. This step aims to: Create and lay the groundwork for the implementation process. Table 5 lists the activities that take place in this stage are described.

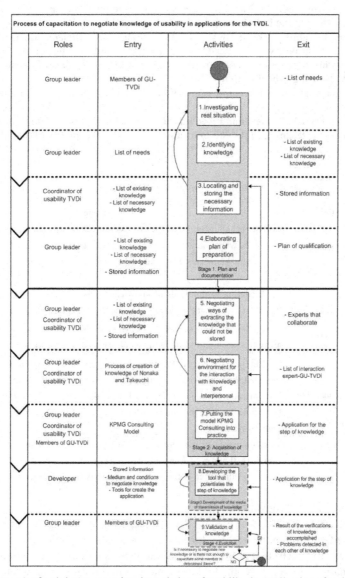

Fig. 2. Process of training to negotiate knowledge of usability in applications for the IDTV.

Table 4. Roles

Leader of GU IDTV: Direct the process of step of a process of training; just like he fulfills the objectives proposed. He should also get the real state from the knowledge of the GU-IDTV and evaluating the functioning of the process.
Coordinator of usability IDTV: He should find reliable and efficient information about the theme of the usability in applications for the IDTV and looking for the best way of representing the information achieving that this is much more accessible for the radio receivers (Appraising role of usability IDTV).
The Developer that the intervening midway elaborates which is going to evidence the information.
Tester of usability IDTV: He should feed on the knowledge that they put at your disposal. It has to target for learning to the full to be able to measure the quality of the software.

Table 5. Activities of the Stage 1.

Activities	Description
Researching the real situation	The real situation in the area of usability is investigated in applications for the IDTV where he goes away to work with the aim of knowing which ones they are the knowledge that take of the theme and the objectives to have in account.
Identifying knowledge	According to the needs of knowledge that exist and the priority of these, they classify the same for the importance that they represent.
Localizing and storing the necessary information	**Taking into account all the deficiencies as to existing knowledge he goes away to search and to store the whole necessary information.**
Do the training plan	**One plans the way that he goes away to implant the system of step of knowledge about proofs, giving your main responsibilities to everyone and the duration of the same. With all these data comes true a chronogram of the whole process, the one for which each role to realize should be directed your work.**
Diagnosing	**A diagnosis to the members of the group to investigate the real situation with the aim of knowing which ones comes true they are the knowledge that they take in the theme of usability in applications for the IDTV.**

Stage 2. Knowledge acquisition

Exist the tacit knowledge of experts. By this stage the knowledge becomes explicit for be stored and to complete the information that exists. Is implemented the model KPMG Consulting [10] that helps to analyze the factors affecting the learning, and to seek alternatives to improve them. Furthermore, conditions and environments are created to manage knowledge. The objectives of this stage are: 1) Define the missing information to obtain; because it is not stored, 2) Manage the interactions between expert and the population, and 3) Put in practice the model KPMG Consulting [10].

Table 6. Activities of stage 2.

Activities	Description
Manage ways to extract knowledge that could not be stored	**Exist information that cannot be collected by means such as Internet or books, because it depends on the experience of experts who are inside or outside the organization. This activity searching forms to contact these experts and analyze the ways in which they are to provide the necessary information. These forms, defined as an interaction between expert and population is planned in time and their execution is controlled.**
Manage the environment for interaction with knowledge and between people.	**Within an organization, each activity has an environment and a moment at which it develops. Search and planning an environment where people can interact with knowledge is not an easy work, because it requires changes and planning. This activity is responsible for managing the environment and conditions that facilitate the creation of new knowledge; for it is based on knowledge creation processes defined by Nonaka and Takeuchi [11] as well as the conditions and environments conducive to learning defined by Nonaka and Konno.**
Implement the model KPMG Consulting.	**The KPMG Consulting model [10] provides factors that influence the learning process of an organization and the results that it produces. This activity makes an analysis of each of these factors and searches the ways to improve them. This may include changes in the forms of managing knowledge. At the end, is performed an evaluation of the implementation of the model KPMG Consulting.**

Stage 3. Development of the means of transmission of knowledge

At this stage, you have the knowledge that must managed and have defined the way to socialize, externalize, combine them and internalize, so you must to design an application that enhances ways to generate, transmit, motivate, develop and acquire new and old knowledge. The objectives of this stage are: 1) Choose the best way to represent information and create a standard that ensures a work uniform and complete, 2 works) select tools that you will use to develop the means for displaying information and facilitate knowledge management.

Stage 4. Evaluation

After the capacitating process is implanted, is necessary to monitor and evaluate the acquired knowledge. The aim of the stage is: 1) validate the knowledge acquired by the GU IDTV.

As mentioned above, the process works in an iterative and growing way. The iteration plan aims to guide the roles in the continuity of the activities and tasks to fulfill. In each iteration must pass for all stages and to realize the priority activities that are or have been pending from previous iterations. It will iterate as many times as necessary in light of that knowledge must be increasing and ways of managing knowledge must be increasingly complete. This process must be constantly monitored to update the information and use new methodologies, methods and tools that can be used to further iterations.

Table 7. Activities of stage 4.

Activities	Description
Validation of knowledge	The Knowledge Management System requires valid feedback because the population is learning as desired, in case of problems or disagreements; measures are taken to improve yourself.

2.5   System for the Management of Heuristic Evaluations

When he began to apply over the procedures explained ahead of time the evaluations were coming true of manual way, which made the process of evaluation difficult, some of these problems show up from now on:

• Inexistence of an automatic controlee of the work realized and human resources that they find available.

• The generation of the checklist to be used for the Coordinators of Usability IDTV was a complex task because they should have selected of a list of indicators that correspond to the characteristics of the appliance to be evaluated.

• The allowance Coordinating of Usability IDTV and Tester of Usability IDTV in a determined evaluation did not have total success of efficient way because the workload was not balanced because there was not an efficacious controlee of the same.

• There did not exist reports that evidence the follow-up of the work accomplished by the testers.

• The controlee of the step of the needs of training does not come true of efficient way.

• There are not efficient mechanisms to get the knowledge of the experts in IDTV across to the reviewers.

• Waste of time and resources (due to this a good step in the conciliation of them cannot be done).

These deficiencies increased to faults in the process of training to negotiate knowledge of usability in applications for the IDTV and in the process of heuristic Evaluations in applications the risks, which did not make possible the reuse of good practices.

By reason of the problems described early was designed a tool that computerizes and automates both processes.

The users that operate the application will have the following roles:

Role	Description
Leader of group	He is responsible for the administration of the system.
Coordinator of Usability	He is in charge of generating and to provide all the necessary elements for the evaluation.
Tester of Usability	They are the persons in charge of accomplishing the evaluation of the system.
Experts	The users with experiences they will take upon themselves to supply knowledge on the area of IDTV.
Team of Development	They are the persons in charge of requesting the evaluation of the product and providing all technical elements for the evaluation.

This tool facilitates the work of the reviewers and consists of 3 fundamental modules:

Module	Administration
Description	Module entrusted to the administration of the necessary basic components to computerize processes.
Roles that Operate	Leader of Group

Principal Functionalities
- a. **Negotiating User**
- b. **Negotiating Roles**
- c. **Negotiating Indicating**
- d. **Negotiating Type of Appliances**
- e. **Negotiating sub-characteristic of usability**

Module	Evaluation
Description	Module in charge of negotiating all the elements that are described in detail to accomplish the heuristic evaluation.
Roles that Operate	Coordinator of Usability, Tester of Usability, Team of Development.

Principal Functionalities
- a. Negotiating Projects.
- b. Assigning Coordinator of the Usability to a determined evaluation.
- c. Assigning Testers of Usability.
- d. Generating List of Indicators.
- e. Accomplishing Evaluation.
- f. Negotiating No Conformities.
- g. Evaluation Issue.

Module	Investigation
Description	Module that takes care of the step of the knowledge of all the members of the Group of Usability. In this module the realized investigations will be publish, already be external or properly of the group. They will guide the trainings specialized for each member of the group. Furthermore, the experts those are external to the group of usability can back up and offering to the knowledge of the components of the group of usability.
Roles that Operate	Group leader, Coordinator of Usability, Tester of Usability and Experts.

Principal Functionalities
- a. Forum
- b. Publishing (comments)
- c. Repository
- d. Negotiating themes of training

Module	Reports
Description	Module in charge to generate reports on all the relevant information of the process of evaluation.
Roles that Operate	Group leader and Coordinator of Usability.
Principal Functionalities	

a. Report of testers assigned to a project.
b. Report of projects for tester.
c. No Conformities report for Tester in a same evaluation.
d. Reports of No Conformities for Evaluation.
e. Report of indicators evaluated by sub-characteristic.
f. Report of total sum of No Conformities for type, in a status of dates.
g. Report of number of No Conformities for evaluation, in a status of dates.
h. Report of number No Conformities for guy, for evaluation.
i. Abearance of the evaluation of sub-characteristic for reviewer.
j. Abearance of the evaluation of sub-characteristic for evaluation.
k. Report of significant No Conformities and No significant for evaluation.
l. Significant report of No Conformities and No significant for evaluation in range of dates.

It is pertinent to stand out that there are integrations between several modules; the most significant is in the module evaluation and investigation. All the indicators registered in the system will have an item related on the forum, this facilitates training online of the reviewers since when they are evaluating an indicator knowledge can deepen be not wanted the same on the set and besides you can ask for help the experts that meet connected upon the evaluation.

3   Conclusions

Based on current trends on digital television applied to the characteristics of the products developed in Cuba of this kind a strategy was defined to perform heuristic evaluations for IDTV applications. It consists of 4 stages which in turn are composed of activities and roles involved with their respective responsibilities.

As part of the activities to be developed to perform heuristic evaluations and the need to train resources human experts on issues of usability applied to the IDTV, within the strategy, a training process was established to manage knowledge in a way that can be obtained, stored, transferred and it is accessible.

The knowledge management system presented in this research is being applied today in the DEPS, the results of its feasibility and best practices that yields will be exposed in future work.

References

1. Bates, P.J.: A study into TV-based interactive learning to the home. PJB Associates, UK. This study has been conducted with funding from the European Community under the IST Program (1998-2003). http://www.pjb.co.uk/...learning/t-learning%20Final%20Report% 20-%20Key%20Highlights%2005-05-03.doc
2. Nielsen, J., Mack, R.L.: Usability Inspection Methods. ISBN: 0471018775, 9780471018773. Digitized: (20 – 11, 2007). p. 413, University of Michigan (1994)
3. González, A.C., et al. : Plataforma de televisión informativa, PRIMICIA. En anales del Festival Internacional de Radio y Televisión, Taller: Rutas de las tecnologías: una mirada desde las Ciencias Informáticas (Habana, Cuba, 2013). Universidad de Ciencias Informáticas (UCI) / Cuba (2013)
4. Pacheco Jerez, Y.S. et al.: Sistema de gestión y transmisión de contenidos audiovisuales, (SIAV). En anales del Festival Internacional de Radio y Televisión, Taller: Rutas de las tecnologías: una mirada desde las Ciencias Informáticas (Habana, Cuba, 2013). Universidad de Ciencias Informáticas (UCI) / Cuba (2013)
5. Góngora Rodríguez, A.E., et al.: Descripción de las clasificaciones de las No Conformidades en un proceso de pruebas de liberación. En anales del VI Congreso Internacional de Ingeniería de Software, Sistemas de Información y Telecomunicaciones; Taller: Peruano de Ingeniería de Software (V WPISBD), (Trujillo, Perú, Noviembre 16 al 21, 2009). Universidad de Ciencias Informáticas (UCI), Cuba (2009)
6. Jessup, G.: Outcomes: NVQs and the emerging model of education and training. Publisher by Falmer Press, London (1991). ISBN ISBN: 1-85000-972-4
7. Fernández Del Monte, Y., et al.: Capacitación orientada a eliminar deficiencias en el aprendizaje. Sistema de gestión de conocimientos. En anales del 7mo. Congreso Internacional de Educación Superior "Universidad 2010"; VII Taller Internacional de Pedagogía de la Educación Superior y Actividad especial: III Simposio "La educación médica: retos y perspectiva, (La Habana, Cuba, Febrero 8 al 12, 2010) (2010). www.contua.org/noticias/ Prog_univ2010.pdf
8. Losa, S., Pañeda, V., Suárez, J.A., Bermejo, C.: La Televisión Digital Interactiva. https://www.yumpu.com/es/document/view/10869591/la-television-digital-interactiva
9. Collazos Ordoñez, C.A., Arciniegas Herrera, J.L.: Evaluación de la televisión interactiva desde una perspectiva de usabilidad: Caso práctico. Revista Ciencia e Ingeniería Neogranadina 19(1), 99–106 (2009). Universidad Militar Nueva Granada, Colombia. http://www. redalyc.org/articulo.oa?id=91113004006
10. Tejedor, y Aguirre: Modelo de Gestión del Conocimiento (1998). http://www.oocities.org/ es/freddymacedo/gercon/modeloKPMG.htm
11. Nonaka. y Takeuchi: Gestión del Conocimiento. Modelo de creación del conocimiento. Teoría de creación del conocimiento por Nonaka. y Takeuchi (1999). http://es.wikibooks. org/wiki/Gesti%C3%B3n_del_conocimiento/Modelo_de_creaci%C3%B3n_del_Conocimi ento/Teor%C3%ADa_de_creaci%C3%B3n_de_conocimiento_por_Nonaka_y_Takeuchi
12. Cobo Romaní, C.: Organización de la información y su impacto en la usabilidad de las tecnologías interactivas. Tesis Programa de Doctorado. Facultad de Ciencias de la Comunicación de la Universidad Autónoma de Barcelona. Departamento de Comunicación Audiovisual y Publicidad. Ciudad de México, México (2005). http://catedragc.mes.edu.cu/download/Tesis %20de%20Doctorado/Ingeniera%20Industrial%20-%20Internacionales/CristobalCoboRoma ni1.pdf

13. Collazos Ordoñez, C.A., Solano, A., Rusu, C., Arciniegas, J.: Evaluating interactive digital television applications through usability heuristics. Revista Chilena de Ingeniería **21**(1), 16–29 (2013). http://www.scielo.cl/scielo.php?script=sci_arttext&pid=S0718-3305201 3000100003

14. Mascheroni, M.A., Greiner, C.L., Dapozo, G., Estayno, M.: Ingeniería de Usabilidad. Una Propuesta Tecnológica para Contribuir a la Evaluación de la Usabilidad del Software. Revista Latinoamericana de Ingeniería de Software **1**(4), 125–134 (2013). ISSN 2314-2642, http://sistemas.unla.edu.ar/sistemas/redisla/ReLAIS/relais-v1-n4-p-125-134.pdf.

15. Paz Espinoza, F.A.: Heurísticas de Usabilidad para sitios web transaccionales: Tesis para optar el grado de Magíster en Informática con mención en Ingeniería de Software. Pontificia Universidad Católica del Perú. Escuela de posgrado. Lima, Perú (2013). http://tesis.pucp.edu.pe/repositorio/handle/123456789/5399

16. Otaíza Fuentes, R.A.: Metodología de Evaluación de Usabilidad para Aplicaciones Web Transaccionales. 2008. Tesis de Grado. Magíster en Ingeniería Informática. Pontificia Universidad Católica de Valparaíso. Facultad de Ingeniería. Escuela de Ingeniería Informática. Valparaíso, Chile (2008)

IDTV Accesibility and Usability

Accessibility: An Open Issue in the Interactive Digital Television

Francisco Montero[✉], Víctor López-Jaquero, and Pascual González

LoUISE Research Group, Escuela Superior de Ingeniería Informática,
Universidad de Castilla-La Mancha, 02071, Albacete, Spain
{fmontero,victor,pgonzalez}@dsi.uclm.es

Abstract. The growing demand of interactive Digital TeleVision (iDTV) is huge, given its potential ability to provide highly personalized services and to access the Web. However these advantages can be missed by difficulties of using it, especially accessibility barriers. This paper analyses interactive digital TV accessibility in a technical level, considering web accessibility context. In addition, it identifies sources of good practices and lessons learned that can improve the accessibility of the applications for the iDTV.

Keywords: Accessibility · Interaction · iDTV

1   Introduction

Television provides an efficient way of gaining access to information and entertainment. Television is also important for enhancing national identity and can be critical in times of emergencies. As an almost universally used technology, TV should be accessible to everyone to avoid discrimination and exclusion. Different accessibility options that enable users to fully access audiovisual content have been in use for a number of years. Traditionally, the most common access services for television have been subtitling, visual signing and audio description. The switch over from analogue to Digital broadcasting brings along a pallet of new opportunities and challenges to provide enhanced access to television [6, 15].

"Access service" or "Accessibility service" is a generic term used to refer to a service (e.g. captioning, audio description etc.) that improves the accessibility of a television program for which it was made. Broadly speaking we can make a distinction between two kinds of access-services depending on whether they are visible to all-viewers (open) or are optional (closed).

There are international and national laws and practices related with accessible DTV. Audio visual media are covered in article 9 of the United Nations Convention on the Rights of Persons with Disabilities (CRDP) states that [21] "To enable persons with disabilities to live independently and participate fully in all aspects of life, States Parties shall take appropriate measures to ensure to persons with disabilities access, on an equal basis with others, to the physical environment, to transportation, to information and communications, including information and communications technologies

© Springer International Publishing Switzerland 2015
M.J. Abásolo and R. Kulesza (Eds.): jAUTI 2014, CCIS 389, pp. 105–119, 2015.
DOI: 10.1007/978-3-319-22656-9_8

and systems, and to other facilities and services open or provided to the public, both in urban and in rural areas."

In its article 30.1.B. the Convention on the Rights of Persons with Disabilities (CRDP) explicitly stipulates that [21] "States Parties recognize the right of persons with disabilities to take part on an equal basis with others in cultural life, and shall take all appropriate measures to ensure that persons with disabilities: Enjoy access to television programs, films, theatre and other cultural activities, in accessible formats.

However, additional improvements can be considered in the current tendencies in the design of applications for the iDTV. This paper reviews this scenario focusing on the accessibility issues. First, Nested Context Language (NCL) is analysed and shortcomings are identified. Later, Web accessibility, HTML5, and Web accessibility Initiative (WAI)-Accessible Rich Internet Application (ARIA) facilities are reviewed in order to identify good practices, lessons learned and recommendations to design accessible interfaces for the iDTV. Finally, conclusions and future works are identified.

2   Nested Context Language

Nested Context Language (NCL) [2, 20] is a declarative language, indeed an XML application, which has been specified in a modular way, aiming at combining its modules into language profiles.

Among the NCL profiles are those targeting digital TV domain. The NCL flexibility, its reuse facility, multi-device support [10], application content and presentation adaptability, and mainly, its intrinsic support for easily defining spatio-temporal synchronization among media assets, including those coming from viewer interactions, make NCL an outstanding solution for all kinds of interactive DTV systems [11].

NCL [20] has a stricter separation between application content and structure. NCL does not define any media content itself. Instead, it defines the glue that holds media together in multimedia presentations. Thus, an NCL document only defines how media objects are structured and related in time and space [12].

Therefore, we can have perceptual content, like videos, images, audios, and texts, as NCL media objects. We can also have media objects with imperative code content, like Lua code [13], ECMAScript code, Java code, etc. In addition, we can have media objects with declarative code content, like HTML-based code, SVG code, X3D code, SMIL code, NCL code (yes, NCL applications embed other NCL applications), etc. Therefore, NCL does not substitute but embeds other language's applications, relating all objects in time and space in a multiple device distributed presentation [10]. There is a plenty of tools that can help to develop iDTV applications using NCL [9, 12].

However, accessibility NCL features were misunderstood and poorly considered and additional user-centered techniques [15, 16] must be considered. The NCL elements, basic and complementary are gathered and commented in the next section.

Table 1 and Table 2 describe the basic and complementary elements of the NCL [1]. NCL is an XML application language for authoring hypermedia documents, including non-linear TV programs. NCL is based on NCM (Nested Context Model).

The version number of an NCL document consists of a major number and a minor number, separated by a dot. The numbers are represented as a decimal number character string with leading zeros suppressed. These NCL elements deal with the NCL version 3.0 [20]. NCL provides basic and complementary facilities in order to specify user interfaces of iDTV but accessibility is lacked and not supported. Examples of use of these elements can be found in several publications and websites, for instance [19].

Table 1. Basic NCL elements

Elements	Subject	Tags

Basic	Structure and Content	`<ncl>`
		`<head>`
		`<body>`
		`<context>`
		`<media>`

	Interfaces	`<area>`
		`<property>`
		`<port>`

	Linking	`<link>`
		`<linkParam>`
		`<bind>`
		`<bindParam>`

	Connectors	`<connectorBase>`
		`<causalConnector>`
		`<compoundCondition>`
		`<simpleCondition>`
		`<compoundAction>`
		`<simpleAction>`
		`<compoundStatement>`
		`<assessmentStatement>`
		`<attributeAssessment>`
		`<valueAssessment>`
		`<connectorParam>`

	Meta-data	`<meta>` `<metadata>`

Historically and currently accessibility support is based on two main techniques [17]: (i) to provide alternative text for any non-text content, and (ii) to use of semantic markup to properly represent the structure of a user interface. These practices are widely used in web development and it will be discussed in the Section 3, but before an example of NCL application is introduced next.

Table 2. Complementary NCL elements

Elements	Subject	Tags

Complementary	Switches and Rules	`<switch>`
		`<switchPort>`
		`<mapping>`
		`<defaultComponent>`
		`<descriptorSwitch>`
		`<defaultDescriptor>`
		`<bindRule>`
		`<ruleBase>`
		`<compositeRule>`
		`<rule>`

	Appearance and Lay-out	`<descriptorBase>`
		`<descriptor>`
		`<descriptorParam>`
		`<regionBase>`
		`<region>`

	Transition Effects	`<transitionBase>` `<transition>`

	Importation	`<importBase>`
		`<importedDocumentBase>`
		`<importNCL>`

3   Web Accessibility: A Tool for Looking at Ourselves

The accessibility recommendations, guidelines and good practices are organized around four principles, which lay the foundation necessary for anyone to access and use Web content. Anyone who wants to use the Web must have content that is [18]:

— Perceivable. Information and user interface components must be presentable to users in ways they can perceive. This means that users must be able to perceive the information being presented.
— Operable. User interface components and navigation must be operable. This means that users must be able to operate the interface.
— Understandable. Information and the operation of user interface must be understandable. This means that users must be able to recognize the information as well as the operation of the user interface.
— Robust. Content must be robust enough that it can be interpreted reliably by a wide variety of user agents, including assistive technologies. This means that users must be able to access the content as technologies advance (as technologies and user agents evolve, the content should remain accessible)

If any of these accessibility principles are not true, users with disabilities will not be able to use the Web.

In WCAG 2.0 under each of the previous principles are guidelines and success criteria that help to address these principles for people with disabilities [18]. Many of these guidelines and success criteria are based on the incorporation of semantic information and description.

3.1 Semantic Sectioning HTML5

HTML5 is the recent specification for HTML, and many browsers are going to start supporting it in the future [3]. One nice thing about HTML5 is that it attempts to stay backwards compatible. But HTML5 is not just about making existing markup shorter. It also introduced a number of new semantic elements. The following elements were defined by the HTML5 specification [3]:

— `<section>` The section tag represents a generic section of a document or application. A section, in this context, is a thematic grouping of content, typically with a heading. A website's home page could be split into different sections for the introduction, news items, and contact information.
— `<nav>` The nav tag represents a section of a page that links to other pages or to parts within the page: a section with navigation links. Only sections that consist of major navigation blocks are appropriate for the nav element.
— `<article>` The article tag represents a self-contained composition in a document, page, application, or site that is intended to be independently distributable or reusable, e.g., in syndication. In a website, an article can be a forum post, a magazine or newspaper article, a blog entry, a user-submitted comment, an interactive widget, or any other independent item of content.
— `<aside>` The aside element represents a section of a page that consists of content that is tangentially related to the content around the aside element, and that could be considered separate from that content. Such sections are often represented as sidebars in printed typography. The element can be used for typographical effects like pull quotes or sidebars, for advertising, for groups of nav elements, and for other content that is considered separate from the main content of the page.
— `<hgroup>` The hgroup element represents the heading of a section. This element is used to group a set of h1–h6 elements when the heading has multiple levels, such as subheadings, alternative titles, or taglines.
— `<header>` The header element represents a group of introductory or navigational aids. A header element is usually intended to contain the section's heading (an h1–h6 element or an hgroup element), but this is not required. The header element can also be used to wrap a section's table of contents, a search form, or any relevant logos.
— `<footer>` The footer element represents a footer for its nearest ancestor sectioning content or sectioning root element. A footer typically contains information about its section such as who wrote it, links to related documents, copyright data, and the like. Footers don't necessarily have to appear at the end of a section, though they usually do. When the footer element contains entire sections, they represent appendixes, indexes, long colophons, verbose license agreements, and other such content.

— `<time>` The time element represents either a time on a 24-hour clock or a precise date in the proleptic Gregorian calendar, optionally with a time and a time zone offset.
— `<mark>` The mark element represents a run of text in one document marked or highlighted for reference purposes.

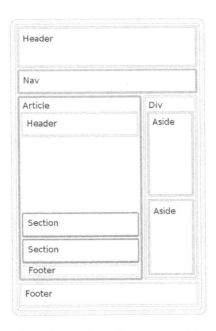

Fig. 1. Example of use of semantic sectioning HTML5 (adapted from [23])

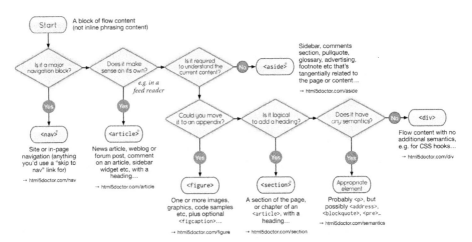

Fig. 2. HTML5 Element flowchart (adapted from [22])

Figure 1 and Figure 2 show, respectively, an example of use of previous semantic sectioning HTML5 and a flowchart to illustrate how some of these HTML5 semantic tags are selected.

3.2   Accessibility and WAI-ARIA

Accessibility of web content requires semantic information about widgets, structures, and behaviours, in order to allow assistive technologies to convey appropriate information to persons with special needs [4, 5, 7, 8, 14]. WAI-ARIA [17] provides ontology of roles, states, and properties that define accessible user interface elements and can be used to improve the accessibility and interoperability of web content and applications. These semantics are designed to allow an author to properly convey user interface behaviours and structural information to assistive technologies in document-level markup.

Complex web and rich internet applications; and iDTV applications may be a good example, become inaccessible when assistive technologies cannot determine the semantics behind portions of a document or when the user is unable to effectively navigate to all parts of it in a usable way. WAI-ARIA proposes to divide the semantics into roles, and states and properties supported by the roles.

Designers and developers need to associate elements in the document to a WAI-ARIA role and the appropriate states and properties (aria-* attributes) during its development, unless the elements already have the appropriate implicit WAI-ARIA semantics for states and properties. In these instances the equivalent host language states and properties take precedence to avoid a conflict while the role attribute will take precedence over the implicit role of the host language element.

The following roles identify structures that organize content in a web page [17]:

— article. A section of a page that consists of a composition that forms an independent part of a document, page, or site.
— columnheader. A cell containing header information for a column.
— definition. A definition of a term or concept.
— directory. A list of references to members of a group, such as a static table of contents
— document. A region containing related information that is declared as document content, as opposed to a web application.
— group. A set of user interface objects which are not intended to be included in a page summary or table of contents by assistive technologies.
— heading. A heading for a section of the page.
— img. A container for a collection of elements that form an image.
— list. A group of non-interactive list items.
— listitem. A single item in a list or directory.
— math. Content that represents a mathematical expression.
— none. An element whose implicit native role semantics will not be mapped to the accessibility API. See synonym presentation.

— `note`. A section whose content is parenthetic or ancillary to the main content of the resource.
— `presentation`. An element whose implicit native role semantics will not be mapped to the accessibility API. See synonym none
— `region`. A large perceivable section of a web page or document, that is important enough to be included in a page summary or table of contents, for example, an area of the page containing live sporting event statistics.
— `row`. A row of cells in a grid.
— `rowgroup`. A group containing one or more row elements in a grid.
— `rowheader`. A cell containing header information for a row in a grid.
— `separator`. A divider that separates and distinguishes sections of content or groups of menuitems.
— `toolbar`. A collection of commonly used function buttons or controls represented in compact visual form.

Moreover, the following roles are regions of a web page intended as navigational landmarks [17]:

— `application`. A region declared as a web application, as opposed to a web document.
— `banner`. A region that contains mostly site-oriented content, rather than page-specific content.
— `complementary`. A supporting section of the document, designed to be complementary to the main content at a similar level in the DOM hierarchy, but remains meaningful when separated from the main content.
— `contentinfo`. A large perceivable region that contains information about the parent document.
— `form`. A landmark region that contains a collection of items and objects that, as a whole, combine to create a form. See related search.
— `main`. The main content of a document.
— `navigation`. A collection of navigational elements (usually links) for navigating the document or related documents.
— `search`. A landmark region that contains a collection of items and objects that, as a whole, combine to create a search facility. See related form.

Figure 3 shows an example of how an HTML5 page might be structured using ARIA landmark roles.

WAI-ARIA puts on the table the need of semantic annotation in web development, but these ideas can be considered also in iTVD. It is expected that, over time, host languages will evolve to provide semantics for objects that currently can only be declared with WAI-ARIA. The main goal of WAI-ARIA is to help stimulate the emergence of more semantic and accessible markup. When native semantics for a given feature become available, it is appropriate for designers and developers to use the native feature and stop using WAI-ARIA for that feature. Legacy content may continue to use WAI-ARIA, however, so the need for user agents to support WAI-ARIA remains.

While specific features of WAI-ARIA may lose importance over time, the general possibility of WAI-ARIA to add semantics to web pages is expected to be a persistent need. Host languages may not implement all the semantics WAI-ARIA provides, and various host languages may implement different subsets of the features. New types of objects are continually being developed, and one goal of WAI-ARIA is to provide a way to make such objects accessible, because web authoring practices often advance faster than host language standards. In this way, WAI-ARIA and host languages both evolve together but at different rates.

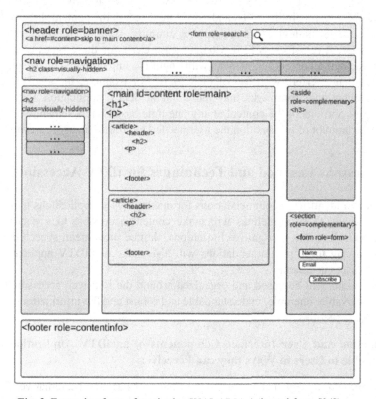

Fig. 3. Example of use of sectioning WAI-ARIA (adapted from [24])

Some languages exist to create semantics for features other than the user interface. For example, SVG expresses the semantics behind production of graphical objects, not of user interface components that those objects may represent; XForms provides semantics for form controls and does not provide wider user interface features. Host languages such as these might, by design, not provide native semantics that map to WAI-ARIA features. In these cases, WAI-ARIA could be adopted as a long-term approach to add semantic information to user interface components. In iDTV application development and its related languages, such as NCL, can adopt also WAI-ARIA facilities.

3.3   Accessibility and Assistive Technologies

Programmatic access to accessibility semantics is essential for assistive technologies [25]. Most assistive technologies interact with user agents, like other applications, through a recognized accessibility API. All important objects in the user interface are exposed to assistive technologies as accessible objects, defined by the accessibility API interfaces. To do this properly, accessibility information needs to be conveyed to the assistive technologies.

Accessibility can be achieved in two main ways: some assistive technologies interact with these accessibility APIs, and others may access the content directly from the DOM. These technologies can restructure, simplify, style, or reflow the content to help a different set of users [25]. Common use cases for these types of adaptations may be the aging population, persons with cognitive impairments, or persons in environments that interfere with use of their tools. For example, the availability of regional navigational landmarks may allow for an iDTV application adaptation that shows only portions of the content at any one time based on its semantics. This could reduce the amount of information the user needed to process at any one time.

4   Lessons Learned and Techniques for iDTV Accessibility

This section identifies recommendations for making iDTV applications more accessible. Following these guidelines will make content accessible to a wider range of people with disabilities, cognitive limitations, limited movement, speech disabilities, etc. Following these recommendations will also make our iDTV applications more usable to users in general.

Suggestions will be based and organized around the four web accessibility principles: perceivable, operable, understandable and robust and the information gathered in the previous sections.

Information and User Interface Components of an iDTV Application must be Presentable to Users in Ways they can Perceive:

— All non-text content that is presented to the user has a text alternative. Especially `media` NCL elements must to have a description of the non-text content. These descriptions can be added as a `property` of `media` elements. However, if `media` NCL elements are pure decoration, is used only for visual formatting, then it is implemented in a way that it can be ignored by assistive technology.
— All time-based media content presented to the user has a text alternative. Captions, audio-only, video-only, lua objects and media alternative must be considered with `media` elements. Property element can include this text alternative. Suggestions related to this issue are: provide a full text transcript of the video and provide a version of the video with audio description
— All media with audio has captions. Adding captions to a video is a relatively hard task, compared to something like writing a text transcript or providing alternative text. Captions must be synchronised with the video to be useful, which means

marking up the plain text with timestamps. There are many free programs that will attempt to create caption file. Moreover, alternative version of video with a sign language interpreter embedded and `link` to it from near the original content can be also considered.

— Create iDTV content that can be presented in different ways without losing information structure. `Switch` element allows for defining alternative objects to be presented and can be used for this purpose. The choice is made during presentation time.

— The content of an iDTV application must be easy to see and hear including separating foreground and background. Colour will not be used as the only visual means of conveying information. In this sense, a light background and dark text or a dark background and light text are two common solutions. Moreover, colour contrast checker tools must be used in order to test the combinations of colours. Using colour is mainly a case of using your common sense: (i) instructions must not rely on colour alone and (ii) other information must not rely on colour alone.

— If an iDTV application has content in a different language to the main language, the change should be identified (`property` tag can be used). This helps users who use assistive technology to understand the full content (text and media elements).

Make all Functionality in iDTV Applications Available from a Remote Control or Keyboard:

— All functionality of the content is operable through a remote control or keyboard interface. All parts of our iDTV application must pass keyboard accessibility. That means forms, menus, buttons, links and everything between. On top of that, specific timings cannot be required for keystrokes to access any feature on the iDTV application.

— Provide users enough time to read and use content. Be careful when you set time limits on your iDTV applications. Some users will need longer than others to read and understand the information. Connectors and Transition effects NCL elements have timing adjustable.

— Flashing users is a bad idea, especially if any of they have epilepsy. To make iDTV applications as safe as possible for all of users, flashing media must be limited. Transition effects and appearance and layout NCL elements will not be used in a way that is known to cause seizures. iDTV applications must not contain anything that flashes more than three times in any one second period.

— iDTV applications provide ways to help users navigate, find content and determine where they are, for instance, screen titled, focus order, area and region headings, labels, and link or connector purpose. In this sense `area` NCL elements must be especially documented to help users and purposes and orders, for instance, should be specified.

Information and the Operation of User Interface must be Understandable:

— iDTV applications keep navigation menus in the same location on all contexts. Present the options in navigation menus in the same order on all contexts and Keep all other standard elements (for instance, search box) in the same location on all contexts.
— The purpose of any `area` in iDTV application must be clear. In this sense, we can learn from semantic sectioning HTML5 (see Section 3.1 and 3.2). HTML5 proposed a semantic markup to describe an element's content. Using semantic markup doesn't provide any immediate benefits to the user, but it does simplify the design of HTML pages. iDTV applications can benefit from suggested semantic markup and assistive technologies can provide aids to the end users. Purposes and orders of areas can be specified by using properties.
— `Link` text must make it clear where the link is going, in the context of their surrounding content. The purpose of the link is clear from the link text, the purpose of the link is clear from the surrounding content and if an image is a link, the alt text of the image makes the link purpose clear
— Any icons used in our iDTV application must be consistent (for example, Twitter of Facebook links).
— Elements in iDTV applications with the same function must be labelled consistently and elements with the same function must be named consistently. Make context appear and operate in predictable ways. Navigational mechanisms that are repeated on multiple contexts occur in the same relative order each time they are repeated.
— Help users avoid and correct mistakes. Labels or instructions are provided when content requires user input. If an input error is automatically detected and suggestions for correction are known, then the suggestions are provided to the user. All submissions of data in our iDTV applications must be checked for input errors and the user is given a chance to correct any mistakes
— Context-sensitive help must be available in our iDTV applications.

Content must be Robust Enough that it can be Interpreted Reliably:

— Maximize compatibility with current and future assistive technologies, such as technologies related to eye-typing, voice, movement, etc.
— Identify, review and use accessibility tools and learn from success accessibility web stories.
— For all interface elements, including links and connectors, the name and role can be programmatically determined; states, properties and values that can be set by the user can be programmatically set and notification of changes to these items is available to assistive technologies.

A set of useful techniques in order to achieve previous principles are gathered in the Table 3.

Table 3. A set of techniques for achieving iDTV accessibility.

Perceivable	T. 1. Providing a movie with extended audio descriptions T. 2. Creating captions for live synchronized media T. 3. Creating content that blinks for less than 5 seconds T. 4. Ensuring that a proper contrast ratio exists between text and background behind the text T. 5. Ensuring that no component of the content flashes more than three times in any one second period T. 6. Placing an alternative for time-based media next to the non-text content. T. 7. Providing a short text alternative that describes the purpose of live audio-only and live video-only content. T. 8. Providing an alternative for time base media. T. 9. Providing a synchronized video for the sign language interpreter that can be displayed in a different viewport on the image by the player T. 10. Providing a version of a movie with audio descriptions T. 11. Using a static text alternative to describe a talking head video. T. 12. Organizing a context using headings T. 13. Using liquid layout
Operable	T. 14. Allowing the content to be paused and restarted from where it was paused T. 15. Allowing users to complete an activity without any time limit T. 16. Playing a sound that turns off automatically within three seconds T. 17. Ensuring keyboard or remote control for all functionality. T. 18. Using semantic markup whenever colour cues are used
Understandable	T. 19. Using semantic elements to mark up structure T. 20. Identifying the purpose of a link using link text combined T. 21. Ordering the content in a meaningful sequence T. 22. Placing the interactive elements in an order that follows sequences and relationships within the content T. 23. Presenting repeated components in the same relative order each time they appear T. 24. Providing text descriptions to identify required fields T. 25. Providing text description when the user provides information that is not in the list of allowed values. T. 26. Providing a text summary that can be understood by people with lower secondary education level reading ability. T. 27. Providing long description for non-text content that serves the same purpose and presents the same information T. 28. Providing descriptive headings T. 29. Providing descriptive labels
Robust	T. 30. Using the accessibility API features of a technology to expose names and roles, to allow user-settable properties to be directly set. T. 31. Using technology that has common-available user agent that support zoom.

5   Conclusions

In this paper we had discussed an open issue in iDTV; accessibility. Accessibility is important not only for individuals and for society; also for governments and for businesses. The main finding and contribution of this work was to identify how available languages, accessibility principles and criteria, and authoring tools can collaborate to produce iDTV contents. The Nested Context Language (NCL) is a widely used language for designing and presenting iDTV applications. However, accessibility issues in iDTV are not addressed till now.

At the same time, web accessibility refers to the inclusive practice of removing barriers that prevent access to websites by people with disabilities. Accessibility of web content requires semantic information about widgets, structures, and behaviours, in order to allow assistive technologies to convey appropriate information to persons with special needs. This paper defends a semantic enrichment of NCL for increasing the accessibility of iDTV applications.

In this paper a set of good practices, lessons learned and techniques for iDTV accessibility improvement were identified from own experience and web development. These recommendations are related to accessibility principles and ergonomic criteria such as perceivable, understandable, operable and robust. NCL, the more extended markup language for iDTV development, lacked some accessibility facilities, such as the ability to manage purposes, captions, orders, useful text alternatives, colours and designate specific sections in the iDTV user interface as the header, navigation, main content, and footer. These elements should be considered in next reviews of this language. NCL and the iDTV development can borrow many success accessibility elements from web development, such as WCAG 2.0 and HTML5. iDTV accessibility improvements are possible by developing a concrete set of accessibility criteria for iDTV and tools for checking its correctness against the accessibility properties.

Acknowledgements. This work has been partially supported by the Red temática en Aplicaciones y Usabilidad de la Televisión digital Interactiva (RedAUTI, Ref. 512RT0461; 2012-2015) and the InsPIre grant (TIN2012-34003; 2013-2015) from the Spanish Government.

References

1. Nested Context Language Handbook. NCL Handbook. http://handbook.ncl.org.br/doku. php?id=ncl. 2012
2. ITU-T Recommendation H.761. Nested Context Language (NCL) and Ginga-NCL for IPTV Services. Geneva, April 2009. http://www.itu.int/rec/T-REC-H.761
3. Pilgrim, M.: HTML5: Up and Running. O'Reilly Media (2010)
4. Francisco-Revilla, L., Crow, J.: Interpretation of web page layouts by blind users. JCDL **2010**, 173–176 (2010)
5. Francisco-Revilla, L., Crow, J.: Interpreting the layout of web pages. Hypertext **2009**, 157–166 (2009)
6. Teixeira, C.A.C., Melo, E.L., Cattelan, R.G., Maria da Graça Campos Pimentel: User-media interaction with interactive TV. In: SAC 2009 pp. 1829–1833 (2009)

7. Luque, V., Delgado, C., Gaedke, M., Nussbaumer, M.: Web Composition with Accessibility in Mind. J. Web Eng. **5**(4), 313–331 (2006)
8. Mankoff, J., Fait, H., Tran, T.: Is your web page accessible?: a comparative study of methods for assessing web page accessibility for the blind. In: CHI 2005, pp. 41–50 (2005)
9. De Albuquerque, R.G., Salles, C., Meireles, M., Costa, R., Alencar, T.: Textual authoring of interactive digital TV applications. In: EuroITV 2011, pp. 235–244 (2011)
10. Monteiro, R., Ferreira, M., Gomes, L.F.: Ginga-NCL: supporting multiple devices. In: WebMedia 2009, p. 6 (2009)
11. Lívio, A., Silva, L.F., Santos de Mattos, F., Nunes, A.P., Bezerra, J.I.; Coelho, C.E., Lemos de Souza, G.: GingaSpace: a solution to execute multidevice applications on broadband TV systems. In: WebMedia 2013, pp. 305–308 (2013)
12. Douglas Paulo de Mattos, D., Varanda da Silva, J., Muchaluat-Saade, D.C: NEXT: graphical editor for authoring NCL documents supporting composite templates. In: EuroITV 2013, pp. 89–98 (2013)
13. Henrique Duarte Bezerra, D., Mariz Timóteo Sousa, D., Lemos de Souza Filho, G., Medeiros Filgueira Burlamaqui, A., Rosberg de Medeiros Silva, I.: Luar: a language for agile development of NCL templates and documents. In: WebMedia 2012, pp. 395–402 (2012)
14. Takagi, H., Saito, S., Fukuda, K., Asakawa, C.: Analysis of navigability of Web applications for improving blind usability. ACM Trans. Comput.-Hum. Interact. **14**(3) (2007)
15. Santana Martins, D., Oliveira, L.S., Campos Pimentel, M.: Designing the user experience in iTV-based interactive learning objects. In: SIGDOC 2010, pp. 243–250 (2010)
16. Piccolo, L.S.G., Melo, A.M., Baranauskas, M.C.C.: Accessibility and interactive TV: design recommendations for the brazilian scenario. In: Baranauskas, C., Abascal, J., Barbosa, S.D.J. (eds.) INTERACT 2007. LNCS, vol. 4662, pp. 361–374. Springer, Heidelberg (2007)
17. W3C. Accessible Rich Internet Applications (WAI-ARIA) 1.1, 12 June, 2014). http://www.w3.org/TR/wai-aria-1.1/. W3c working Draft
18. Jantsch, A., Basso, L.O., Machado, R.P., Santarosa, L.M.C.: Acessibilidade a TVDI e Web: desvelando parámetros de similaridades. Anales de IIJAUTI 2013 : II Jornadas Iberoamericanas de Difusión y Capacitación sobre Aplicaciones y Usabilidad de la Televisión Digital Interactiva, pp. 132–139 (2013)
19. Gomes Soares, L.F., Ferreira Moreno, M., de Salles Soares Neto, C.: Ginga-NCL: Declarative middleware for multimedia IPTV services. IEEE Communications Magazine **48**(6), 74–81 (2010)
20. Gomes Soares, L.F.: Nested Context Language 3.0. Part 13 – Ginga-NCL Implementors guide v1.0. Laboratório TeleMidia DI-PUC-Rio (2009)
21. eAccess+. Legislation for accessible DTV. (2013). http://hub.eaccessplus.eu/wiki/Legislation_for_accessible_Audio-visual_media
22. HTML5 Doctor. Helping you implement HTML5 today. Let's talk about Semantics (2012). http://html5doctor.com/lets-talk-about-semantics/
23. BASE Webmaster. The HTML5 page structure. How to structure pages using the new HTML5 elements (2011). http://www.basewebmaster.com/html/html5-page-structure.php
24. Accessible classroom technologies. HTML5 Accessible code examples. https://carmenwiki.osu.edu/display/10292/HTML5+Accessibility+Code+Examples. 2014
25. W3C. WAI-ARIA 1.0 User Agent Implementation Guide. A user agent developer's guide to understanding and implementing Accessible Rich Internet Applications. W3C Recommendation, 20 March, 2014

Designing a Methodological Process to Identify the Most Suited Recognition Technique for Elderly Users of Interactive TV

Telmo Silva[✉] and Jorge Abreu

University of Aveiro, Campus Universitário Santiago 3810-193, Aveiro, Portugal
{tsilva,jfa}@ua.pt

Abstract. User identification in interactive Television (iTV) is an enthusiastic research area that aims to find the most reliable and non-invasive solution allowing viewers to enjoy a truly personalized TV experience. However, usability and efficiency of recognition methods depend upon users' cognitive and psychomotor characteristics, scenario even more complex when elderly viewers are at stake, since they present a great variety of combinations of those parameters. In this framework, the paper depicts the process that led to a methodology to identify the most suited recognition technique to each specific profile of elderly iTV users. The considered recognition methods were associated to an iTV system designed to promote comfort and sociability among elderly.

In the final setup a Wizard of Oz prototype was used, being participants interviewed at their homes and characterized based on International Classification of Functioning, Disability and Health (ICF). A decision matrix was implemented, enabling to find the best trade-off between elderly's profile and recognition method.

Keywords: Seniors · Research process · iTV · Identification · Usability

1 Introduction

Scientific and technological discoveries change the way of living and organization of societies. These changes occur at different levels and, in most cases, are associated with the leverage of well-being, happiness and comfort. There are many examples of remarkable discoveries in areas as diverse as health, transport and communication. Television is undoubtedly one of these findings [14]. It had a tremendous impact on societies and has been one of the majors socializing agents. It was, and still is, an interesting promoter of conversations, which are sometimes triggered with phrases as "did you saw the game?", "did you saw the "the Voice show?", "What did you think about that program about cars?". If we look at this discovery according to McLuhan's [8] perspective, that everything we create tends to extend human attributes, television prolonging, for example, hearing and speech. For McLuhan "the medium is the message" and thus the mean is as powerful as the way it passes the message.

© Springer International Publishing Switzerland 2015
M.J. Abásolo and R. Kulesza (Eds.): jAUTI 2014, CCIS 389, pp. 120–134, 2015.
DOI: 10.1007/978-3-319-22656-9_9

Currently television is seen as a media paving the way for construction of opinion and knowledge by the masses influencing people' perspectives on values, traditions and standards [23]. Associated with television, the great technological revolution of recent decades is also significantly related to the appearance of personal devices along with the development and spread of the Internet, easing communication through digital technologies.

Of course, the development of a technological infrastructure so extensive as the Internet supports a set of new services, both directly related to its emergence as others who migrated to this new digital paradigm. The television market, like many other media, moved part of its influence to the Internet, first through portals (with information, content streaming, recommendations, etc.) and, secondly, using the Internet as a supporting infrastructure for Over the Top Content distribution. This type of content delivering differs from the traditional TV system since it implies that the viewers have a dedicated connection to a telecom operator allowing a bidirectional information transmission, supporting customization of content and interactive services. Although often be seen as a communication media that is losing influence over the others, a more detailed observation of extended studies allows to see that, even considering a great competition, television continues to play an important role. This is especially relevant when elderly people are at stake, as the research conducted by Nielsen [9] proves, when showing that people over 65 years living in the United States spend approximately 45 hours each week viewing TV and only about 3 hours a week using the Internet. For this target audience, watching TV is a daily routine, being the TV set part of their everyday life. In the same report we can see that, even in younger age groups such as 25 to 34 years, the weekly television consumption ranges in the order of 26 hours and access to Internet in a traditional computer is about 6 hours [9]. In the same study it is possible to confirm the predominance of television against the other communication means.

Supported in this reality (high television consumption in all age groups, but especially among elderly), this work focuses on the process of automatically viewers' identification, a premise toward granting a total personalized TV experience supported on interactive television (iTV) services, including life support services. As a result of the generalized aging of the population, seniors are a target of increasing attention by: i) governments, that apparently began to realize the social weight of this class; ii) care networks, that find themselves forced to manage an increasing number of people, and by iii) the scientific community in various areas.

Concepts of aging, old age, senior, elderly people' health, associated with culture, law and duty are very broad. Its complexity and interconnection, along with objective and subjective components, allows perceiving that research of technological solution devoted to elderly people are necessarily multidisciplinary and interdisciplinary. The feature that is most evident among senior population is its multidimensional characteristics. However, in the discursive and mental lexicon it is being seen systematically and wrongly, as homogeneous.

In this context, this research work, whose target audience are the seniors, considers their specificities (physical, sensory and cognitive), needs and expectations, using interactive television services, in an attempt to characterize the user identification system most suited to a specific user profile. Technologically, there are multiple challenges to address this issue. Adding to the technical problem, the ones related with social, health, wellness, usability and user experience, associated with senior users generates a strong motivation inherent to this work.

Next section of this paper describes the aging process, and then the problem under study is depicted. After, the research process used to solve the problem is explained and finally the conclusions are presented.

2   The Aging Process

Aging is a process that occurs in a different way from person to person, and is characterized by a high variability of capacity levels on cognitive, visual and auditory dimensions. Variations depend among others on medication regimens and fatigue [25].

In the scope of this paper, the relevance of these variations is that they stress the design and development of user interfaces targeted to seniors. As an example, in this framework Zajicek [25] proposed the possibility of switching between different modes of interaction (e.g. voice, text, remote control) to minimize user's fatigue levels, as well to compensate problems associated with visual or cognitive impairments. In addition, seniors also tend to have another transversal characteristic: the aversion to new technologies motivated by fear of failure, leading them to refuse the adoption of digital technologies [5]. There are two more factors that inhibit seniors to use new technologies [25]: i) non-perception of utility; and ii) the apparent huge amount of knowledge needed to use them. We can extrapolate these handicaps in the usage of iTV interfaces because its user interaction paradigms are relatively close, from usage and learning point of views [6].If we look to the changes associated to the aging process, and how they impact on the usage of technologies, it appears that those associated with intellectual abilities related with memory are very important [25]. Zajicek states that the crystalline memory, referring to knowledge already acquired, is not affected. In addition, he refers that the capacity of learning and retention of new knowledge may be affected by aging, e.g. seniors tend to have more difficulty navigating in a route than young people, and the same navigation logic is used, for example, while browsing the Internet. Seniors overcome this by trying to find metaphors in their daily lives to better understand the mechanisms of navigation in interfaces. The aging process also brings a reduction of visual acuity, often not reported because many patients consider it a characteristic of the aging process [16]. In addition, about a third of seniors over 65 years and half of those over 85 years presents hearing problems, mainly caused by presbycusis. This handicap is a result of the aging process affecting ear's structure with a progressive atrophy of the inner ear cochlea.

Associated with this decrease in hearing and visual skills is the risk of social isolation and depression. Nevertheless, treatment with hearing and visual aids can improve social, emotional, communicative and cognitive aspects of seniors' life [16].

Another inherent characteristic of age increase is the limitation on the movement of the shoulders that may appear silently and painlessly, leading to difficulties in executing many daily tasks such as dressing, driving, bathing, sleeping. In addition, this type of limitations also arises at lower limbs, leading to the fact that about one-third of elderly falls at least once each year [1].

3   The Problem

Based on: i) the above outlined seniors' specificities; ii) the technical characteristics of the current interactive television services; iii) and the goal to understand how the automatic identification of senior users in interactive television can be solved - a crucial factor for the development of new personalized services, this paper sets up a research process that seeks to answer the following question:

"What is the most suited recognition method to each specific profile of elderly iTV users providing an adequate usability and user experience?" The theoretical basis proposed by Quivy & Campenhoudt to research projects in the area of social sciences claim that, after the definition of the research question, the researchers should define hypotheses that will be the subject of evaluation [13]. Nevertheless, given the inherent qualitative and evolutionary nature of this work, the research process is supported in the Grounded Theory [19], based on building knowledge from the data collected. The research projects most scalable and qualitative typically uncover concepts and relationships in data collected by drawing up a theoretical framework. This method is based on flexible data, detailed and inseparable from the context, which usually are gathered through words or images especially appropriated to understand the nature of human experience in specific contexts [19]. To assist the knowledge building, "case studies" were also carried, thus combining the two methods (Grounded Theory and "case studies") to find an answer to the research question. According to Carmo and Ferreira [2], this methodological integration promotes a better illustration and understanding of the phenomenon under analysis, allowing the establishment of relations between the obtained results.

4   The Research Process

A research is often a long and complex process, suffering many changes during its life cycle that need to be accommodated using the appropriate methodology.

The research process to achieve the identification of the most suited recognition method to each specific profile of elderly iTV users is described along this text. In its basic form, users' identification systems are based on entering a user name and a password. However, in the domain of interactive television systems (iTV), this basic identification method could not be the most appropriated one, due to the limitations of the input device (the remote control), particularly when users demand a relaxing experience. In this framework, other identification technologies should be considered: i) RFID card and a portable card reader; ii) bracelet with an active marker; iii) automatically face recognition; iv) facial recognition controlled by the user; v) voice recognition (with a microphone placed on the remote); and vi) fingerprint reader placed on the remote.

4.1   Theoretical Framework

In the scientific field of social sciences (and related areas) other approaches than those proposed by Quivy & Campenhoudt [13] can be applied. In many qualitative and practical researches, the Grounded Theory is often adopted due to its empirical basis, stating that the resulting theories are based on the data collected [4]. It comprises a set of methodological procedures that, based on the data collected, allow an integrated and evolutionary analysis of its content, inductively creating knowledge [18]. This methodology comprises a constant comparison of all aspects of the data as a main procedure. Its qualitative nature goes beyond the observation and interview techniques to decode the psycho mechanisms associated to the phenomena under study, building theories based on collected data.

The grounded theory states that building theories can be achieved analysing qualitative data gathered in interviews, observations, written material such as letters or diaries, and even using quantitative techniques. In this methodology there are constructed explanatory frameworks, or theories based on empirical generalizations, that allow the development of explanations applicable to wider contexts. As it is supported on these assumptions, this approach has a different philosophy from the others, because it allows the researcher to do the investigative work without building hypotheses. Contrary to the theories developed by deduction (fulfilling logical, rigid and deductive rules), where hypotheses are confronted with the observations, the grounded theory comprises the inductive construction, namely to develop knowledge supported in data collection. The basis of the grounded theory is the development of data collection processes and the constant discovery of knowledge from the collection procedures and data analysis. The researchers must have an active attitude to start the knowledge building process based on the data collected, during the investigation. This is build knowledge besides of just test a theory. [19] [20].

In the case of this research it should be observed that the Ground Theory was the methodology used to support the gathering of the initial data, both through exploratory interviews and a careful analysis of the state of the art in the research area of automatic users' identification systems in iTV. Additionally to the Grounded Theory, the results obtained in this research were also supported by other methods. The knowledge building was also supported not only in the Ground Theory due to some of its limitations: i) the subjectivity of the data collected, that can lead to difficulties / trust issues on the resulting knowledge; ii) the resulting knowledge can be biased by the researcher; iii) the qualitative results can be difficult to display [19].

Besides the Grounded Theory methodology, others can emerge when the research has an empirical component like development and testing of prototypes where data gathering is crucial to knowledge building. When seeking to understand, explore or describe events in complex contexts, where several factors are involved, a "case study" is the approach at stake [24]. To Yin the "case study" is a methodology to study a phenomenon in its real context, where relationships between its influencing factors and its contexts are not evident [24].

To Yin this approach can be adapted to investigations where the researcher is faced with complex situations in real contexts in which is hard to identify significant variables.

Yin states that this approach can be also adopted in situations where it is necessary to give answers to the "how" and "why", or situations where the researcher seeks to find relationships between factors of the entities involved. According to Yin this approach can be adopted even in investigations where it is necessary to analyse a phenomenon to understand its dynamics and processes. Thus, in summary, Yin sets "case studies" by the features of the phenomena in study, characteristics of the data collection process and the respective data analysis strategies.

For Bell [3], a "case study" is a broad definition for methodologies of research concerned with the relationship between factors and events [3]. To Ponte[17] a "case study" is an particularistic investigation that deliberately study a specific situation that is thought as unique, at least in certain aspects, to find their specific and differentiating characteristics and thus contribute to the overall understanding of a particular phenomenon.

In this research it will be used the definition of Yin to "case study". This definition characterizes the "case study" as a methodology that is concerned with a rich description of events, linking description with its analysis. The focus of attention of a "case study" can be individual actors or groups of actors, and there understanding about the events. For Yin the "case studies" can be conducted under different theoretical frameworks that are not only supported in descriptive and experimental aspects. However, typically, they have an empirical dimension. For the author the "case studies" are related essentially with processes that progress inductively and with a heuristic nature. However, to Yin, a "case study" is not generalizable.

For Yin, there are three types of "case study", according to the purpose of the study: exploratory, explanatory and descriptive. An exploratory "case study" is an initial research trying to find patterns to describe and visualize the data collected. In this kind of research data are gathered in the early stages of researches and then are analysed in order to explain and understand the phenomena. Typically the research questions that motivate a case study of this type are those that focus on the aspects of the phenomenon, such as "What are the techniques to increase sales?". According to the author this kind of "case study" happens when you know very little of the reality under study, resulting in the fact that the data is used to clarify and define the phenomena.

A descriptive "case study" aims to obtain further information on a detail of the phenomenon. This type of "case study" is based on the existence of a theory that allows direct data collection. As in "case study" exploratory, this also focuses on the understanding of a phenomenon, but in this type there is a knowledge base that supports research questions like: "What were the results of using a particular sales technique?". In this kind of "case study" it exist a dense and detailed description of a phenomenon in its natural context.

The explanatory "case studies" are even deeper as they try to analyse and explain the reasons for a phenomenon to happen and how it happens. The research questions focus on the "how" and "why" such as: "why a certain action of promotion leads to increased sales?". In this type of "case study" the researcher tries, based on the data collected in a specific context, to establish cause and effect relations, in order to generate new knowledge.

4.2   Initial Approach

In the first plan draft for this work, it was expected, after a set of exploratory interviews, to develop a functional prototype that would be tested with a group of seniors' users. In these tests it would be able to define the viewer identification system (VIS) more suitable for seniors in the context of iTV applications [15]. The summary of this first plane research is shown in Figure 1.

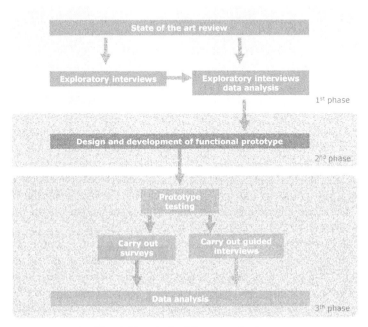

Fig. 1. First draft of the research plan.

This approach tried to answer to the research question (technique defined by Quivy and Campenhoudt [13]) taking advantage from the methodological crossing of the grounded theory, with the "explanatory case study" development (as is defined by Yin). The grounded theory was one of the 1st phase pillars of this process and it allowed to understand all the theory framework of the work to be performed, through of an qualitative analysis of the exploratory interviews and readings more extensive about the seniors' characteristics.

The "case study" performed with the help of the functional prototype, specifically developed for the purpose, intended to better understand the phenomenon under study, as well its sociological framework. This functional prototype allows user to be identified by the iTV system through an RFID card or the activation of a Bluetooth module of, for example, a mobile phone that is with him. As a complement to the prototype test, and subsequent interviews, other forms of identification were proposed to seniors (which were not implemented in the tested prototype) to understand if there was a clear preference trend about the identification system. In these interviews / test, due to the seniors' particularities, it was very difficult to transmit efficiently the idea that could be used other techniques for the users' recognition, particularly those mentioned in section 4 of this text, this factor may have influenced the dispersion in the interviewees' answers. As there was not a clear trend, the sequence and objectives of the work had to be redesigned in order to develop a matrix that allowed to define the most appropriate VIS to a specific use context (e.g. senior with difficulties with fine motor skills, senior with reduced mobility, etc.). Consequently, in order to build / fill this matrix it was necessary to develop a second functional prototype to enable the users' identification across all identification methods (in a total of six - listed in section 4 of this text) which were intended to study.

4.3   Final Approach

After analysing the results of this first exploratory study, it was necessary to redesign the research process to build a decision matrix, which became, after the initial approach, the main objective of this work. Figure 2 summarizes the various stages of development process and represents the consolidated methodology after the exploratory process. The figure also permits a more detailed analysis of each of the stages of the study, featuring the appropriate methodologies to achieve the objectives set out for the job.

Using Figure 2 can be seen that the components described in the previous section (initial approach), (where the main conclusions leading to the consolidated definition of the investigative process were obtained), are, in the new design, the components of the exploratory dimension of this research (1st, 2nd and 3rd stages shown in Figure 2). This new design has two more phases: i) - 4th stage - the design and development of the second prototype (Based on the "Wizard of Oz" concept [7]; and ii) - 5th phase - the "case study" with this "wizard of oz" prototype to collect data to fill the decision matrix created during this investigation.

It is important to refer that in the exploratory dimension of the research (phases 1-3), after the definition of the research question, we used two methodological approaches: Grounded Theory and "case studies"; with this strategy the research team aimed to promote the best illustration and understanding of the phenomena under study, promoting the development and clarification of relations between the collected data [2], in order to create knowledge (see Figure 2). In phase 3 was conducted a "case study" in which data were collected by direct observation and semi-structured interviews. These interviews were conducted at seniors' homes to ensure a relaxed atmosphere. Thus it was possible to gather better data as advocated by Obrist, Bernhaupt and Tscheligi in [10]. The "case study" concept can be applied to this stage because, this technique searches what's essential and specific in the use of VIS prototype (a well-defined study object) [11].

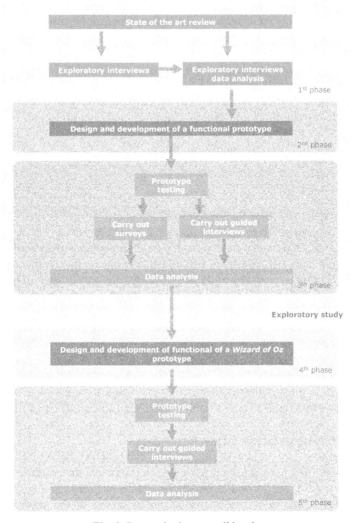

Fig. 2. Research plan consolidated.

In the case of this research it was intended to analyse in what context is that a non-intrusive identification system can be useful to make easier for seniors access to personalized services of interactive television. The study focused in both the technical aspects that feature a user identification system, and in the sociological aspects of its use as the loss of privacy, usability, user experience and wishes and needs of senior users when using interactive television services, which further reinforces the importance of the interviews at homes of potential users.

During this first "case study", the data collected were subjected to a qualitative analysis and also a quantitative analysis. The first "case study" did not produce the desired results for this investigation, so it was necessary to develop 4th and 5th phases. The second "case study" (Phase 5), performed after the conclusions of the exploratory study, it was also an explanatory "case study", as defined by Yin. The data of the tests to the prototype were collected by direct observation and by semi-structured interviews at seniors' homes to ensure an efficient and successful data collection (as already referred). The collected data were analysed in a qualitative way, but also in quantitative away, in order to ensure the development of decision matrix that defines the most appropriate identification system to a particular user profile. Prior to the realization of tests of this last phase of the research and in order to validate the quality of the prototype as well as the quality of the interview guide, it were conducted 5 testing procedures with five people chosen by convenience. These participants, not seniors, were chosen due to their extensive experience in the use of technology and also due to its experience in dealing with seniors.

4.4   Resultant Matrix

Upon completing the exploratory study and from the analysis of the test data and the methodological process developed in this initial part of the research, the work was restructured in order to build a decision matrix that would allow defining the most appropriate VIS to a particular user profile. However, in this phase, a concept is still not detailed: the user profile and the variables / parameters which will define him. In the initial phase of this work, which consisted of the data gathering from: the existing literature, the set of exploratory interviews and the tests with a working prototype, it was found that the physical, cognitive and social skills affect the way how seniors perceive the qualities of each identification technology. Based on these assumptions, it was defined a set of parameters that will allow characterizing the user profiles. The profiles definition used throughout this work is closely related to the ICF classification [22] because this classification is validated by the World Health Organization and allows qualifying multiple aspects of the individuals and, in addition, it is widely accepted in the scientific community. Thus, after having made the data analysis of the third phase of this research, the following characteristics were defined as users' description parameters and consequently as matrix input parameters: i) visual acuity; ii) vocal ability; iii) mobility; iv) digital literacy; v) fine motor skills; vi) hearing acuity; vii) memory. Thus, by measuring the capacity of each person in these parameters it is possible to characterize the user profile. In the case of this work it was used: i) the Jaeger Eye Chart (JEC) test to measure visual acuity; ii) the whisper test to measure hearing acuity; iii) the timed Up & Go test to measure the mobility [12]; iv) the Nine Hole Peg Test to measure fine motor skills; iv) the European Commission Report to measure digital literacy [21]; v) and direct observation to measure memory and vocal ability. After this characterization it was tried to understand how every user profile may be assigned to the most appropriate VIS. In order to fulfill this objective, a methodology was outlined to fill the decision matrix which will allow, for a given set of parameters values that characterize the user, identifying the most appropriate VIS for that user (Figure 4). The idealized methodology was composed by the prototype development that would allow testing the identification technologies under study and by a set of interviews / tests performed at users' home to rate their preferences regarding the identification technology. Based on the findings of the exploratory study, the applied methodology had to consider that it is essential that the prototype to be tested by senior allows the experimentation of all technologies. Technically, to develop a prototype which allows testing a wide range of technologies, both in terms of numbers (6 in total) as development costs that imply is a complex and time-consuming task. Regarding the development cost, it is important to mention that it implies the algorithms development for facial and voice recognition and the integration of several types of hardware, such as video cameras and card readers with active and not active RFID tags. Considering all development costs it is easily understood that, within the available resources and time, it was not possible to develop a high-fidelity prototype that would effectively allow experiencing all the technologies under study. Thus, it was decided to develop a high fidelity prototype based on the Wizard of Oz concept [7] which needs, at the experimentation time, of an individual to control all of its implementation (Figure 3). This approach claims that the prototypes should be developed to ensure the user feels that everything happens as a fully functional and high-fidelity prototype, when in reality, its interaction, which should be carried out automatically by the prototype, is being controlled by another external user. Thus, it is possible to obviate the time required for prototyping and still simulate complex features of the development viewpoint.

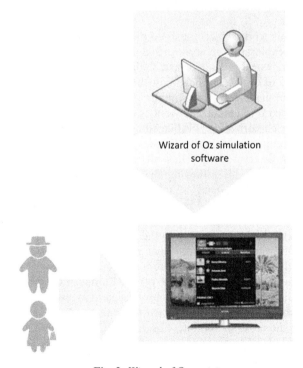

Wizard of Oz simulation software

Fig. 3. *Wizard of Oz* prototype

Considering all these parameters (visual and hearing acuity, etc.) and the metrics defined for each of them, the matrix was developed which, after completed, will serve to decision-making about the most appropriate VIS to a particular user profile, for example by operators or by seniors' caregivers. Thus, the matrix has in its columns the definition parameters of the user profiles and has on its routes the various technologies that can be used for the VIS. The cells have the representation of each identification technology for a given performance, in the parameter of the corresponding column.

To fill the matrix, it was necessary, at the time of the interviews / tests, to evaluate each participant in terms of several considered aspects to characterize the user profile, in order to notice which each of them belongs. In other words, it was necessary, at the time in which the senior tested the prototype, to evaluate also their functional capabilities, such as his mobility. The results of those tests were later analyzed and considered to fill the matrix. Figure 4 depicts the developed matrix.

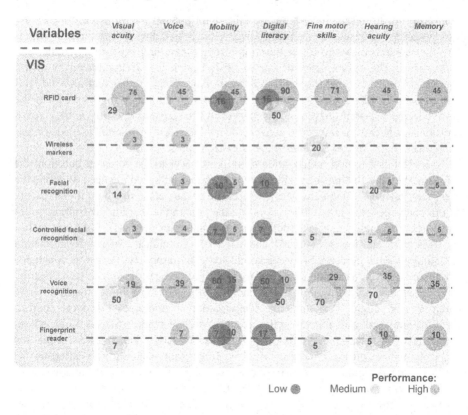

Fig. 4. Decision Matrix

It is important to mention that the data which contains this representation is illustrative only. To understand the matrix representation it is important to clarify some details of its construction. Thus, the performance in each of the measured characteristics is shown in a three-color scale: i) a low performance is represented by the purple color; ii) an average performance is represented by the yellow color; iii) and a good performance by the green color.

In order to facilitate the matrix interpretation we take as an example the case of the digital literacy parameter (based on Figure 4, assuming it represents a completely filled matrix): for individuals with high digital literacy, 90% of them prefer the VIS based on RFID cards and 10% based on voice recognition. To understand this interpretation it is necessary to note that, in Figure 4, there are two green circles associated with the high digital literacy parameter, in which one has a value of 90%, representing the preference percentage associated with the VIS based on RFID card and the other has 10%, associated with the VIS based on voice recognition.

5   Conclusions

Answering to the research question was the main goal of the work described here. This research was based on Grounded Theory, and thus it does not proposed hypotheses. The research answered to the question through literature, exploratory studies and case studies. The consolidated design of this research was characterized by a first phase that consisted in: i) literature review; ii) exploratory studies that allowed realizes all theoretical framework of the study, iii) design a solution that streamlines the answer to the research question. This answer to the research question is based on a decision matrix that for a specific user profile computes the best suited user identification process in the context of interactive television applications.

To build this decision matrix underlying the answer to the research question, the team analysed the findings of preliminary studies that indicated the need to define the user identification system considering the profile of the person to whom it is intended. At this stage the interviews with seniors and the tests to the first high definition prototype were extremely important (both were held at senior's homes). Thus, the matrix was designed considering seniors' characteristics to indicate which identification technology should be used. From the conducted exploratory studies it was concluded that there are seven parameters that influence the preferences of seniors: sight, hearing acuity, memory, speaking ability, fine motor skills, mobility, digital literacy. These parameters are highly related to the identification technologies that were studied: identification card with the respective reader, wireless marker placed on an adornment, always-on facial recognition, controlled facial recognition, speaker recognition with microphone on the remote control and fingerprint scanning also based on the remote. After designing the matrix it was necessary fill it with data in order to be useful. To achieve this goal, a second functional prototype was tested. It should be noted that there was one factor (among others) which was very important to the success in obtaining relevant data for the matrix: the prototype allowed testing all technologies under study. This was only possible because the prototype was developed based on Wizard of Oz concept which allowed simulate all technologies under study. This need was identified during the exploratory study, and specifically during the tests of the first working prototype. In a detached analysis of interactive television and identification systems, the methodology carried out in this research can be applied to many other areas: i) the concept of a decision matrix with input parameters to characterize a user may be suitable for studies that to a profile, decides on a technology, a product or article; ii) the methodological approach that depends on building and testing a prototype in a real environment applies especially when the target audience is elderly; iii) use a set of cognitive and physical parameters to define a user profile is also an approach that can be applied in multiple contexts, such as to define a product for a specific user profile.

References

1. Álvares, L.M., Lima, R.D.C., Silva, R.A.D.: Ocorrência de quedas em idosos residentes em instituições de longa permanência em Pelotas, Rio Grande do Sul, Brasil. Cadernos de Saúde Pública, 2010, 26 (2010)
2. Carmo, H.D.D.A., Ferreira, M.M.D.: Metodologia da investigação:guia para auto-aprendizagem. Universidade Aberta (1998)
3. Fidel, R.: The case study method: A case study. Library and Information Science Research 6(3) (1984)
4. Glaser, B., Strauss, A.: The Discovery of Grounded Theory: Strategies for Qualitative Research. Aldine Publishing Company, Chicago (1967)
5. Gregor, P., Newell, A., Zajicek, M.: Designing for dynamic diversity: interfaces for older people. In: Proceedings of the Fifth International ACM Conference on Assistive Technologies. ACM, Edinburgh, Scotland (2002)
6. Lorenz, A., Oppermann, R.: Mobile health monitoring for the elderly: Designing for diversity. Pervasive and Mobile Computing (2008)
7. Maudsley, D., Greenberg, S., Mander, R.: Prototyping an intelligent agent through Wizard of Oz. CHI 1993 Proceedings of the INTERACT 1993 and CHI 1993 Conference on Human Factors in Computing Systems, pp. 277–284 (1993)
8. McLuhan, M.: The Gutenberg Galaxy: The Making of Typographic Man. University of Toronto Press (1962)
9. Nielsen: The Total Audience Report – Q4, 2014, Nielsen Company (2015)
10. Obrist, M., Bernhaupt, R., Tscheligi, M.: Users@Home: Implications from studying iTV. In: 20th International Symposium on Human Factors in Telecommunication. Sophia-Antipolis, France (2006)
11. Pardal, L., Correia, E.: Métodos e Técnicas de Investigação Social (1995)
12. Podsiadlo, D., Richardson, S.: The timed "Up & Go": a test of basic functional mobility for frail elderly persons. Journal of the American Geriatrics Society 39(2), 8 (1991)
13. Quivy, R., Campenhoudt, L.V.: Manual de Investigação em Ciências Sociais. Gradiva (2005)
14. Ruggiero, T.E.: Uses and Gratifications Theory in the 21st Century. Mass Communication & Society 3(1), 34 (2000)
15. Silva, T., Abreu, J., and Pacheco, O.R.: Sistema multi-modal de identificação de utilizadores IPTV- um processo de investigação. In: Interacção 2010. Aveiro (2010)
16. Silva, T., Abreu, J., Pacheco, O.: Identificação de utilizadores: a chave para a personalização de aplicações de TV interativa para seniores? Communication Studies / Estudos em Comunicação 14, 137–156 (2013)
17. Soar, J., Croll, P.: Assistive technologies for the frail elderly, chronic illness sufferers and people with disabilities – a case study of the development of a smart home. In: Australian Conference on Information Systems. Toowoomba (2007)
18. Strauss, A., Corbin, J.: Basics of Qualitative Research Techniques and Procedures for Developing Grounded Theory, p. 312. Sage Publications, London (1998)

19. Strauss, A. and Corbin, J.: Basics of Qualitative Research: Techniques and Procedures for Developing Grounded Theory. 2 (ed), ed. S. Publications. Sage Publications (1998)
20. Strauss, A., Corbin, J.: Grounded Theory in Practice. Sage Publications (1997)
21. Tornero, J.M.P., Luque, S.G., Paredes, O.: Study on Assessment Criteria for Media Literacy Levels: A comprehensive view of the concept of media and an understanding of how media literacy levels in Europe should be assessed. In: Celot, P. (ed), p. 92. European Commissionk, Brussels. (2009)
22. WHO: International Classification of Functioning, Disability and Health (ICF) - World Health Organization (2001)
23. Wolton, D.: Penser la communication. Flammarion, Paris (1997)
24. Yin, R.: Estudo De Caso: Planejamento E Metodos. Bookman Companhia (2005)
25. Zajicek, M.: Interface design for older adults. In: Proceedings of the 2001 EC/NSF Workshop on Universal Accessibility of Ubiquitous Computing: Providing for the Elderly. 2001, pp. 60–65. Alcácer do Sal, Portugal, ACM (2001)

Usability Study of Gestures to Control a Smart-TV

Silvia Ramis[1], Francisco J. Perales[1(✉)], Cristina Manresa-Yee[1], and Antoni Bibiloni[2]

[1] Group of Computer Graphics, Computer Vision and AI,
Department of Mathematics and Computer Science,
University of Balearic Islands (UIB), Palma de Mallorca, Balearic Islands, Spain
{silvia.ramis,paco.perales,cristina.manresa}@uib.es
[2] Laboratory of Information Technologies and Multimedia (LTIM),
Department of Mathematics and Computer Science,
University of Balearic Islands (UIB), Palma de Mallorca, Balearic Islands, Spain
antoni.bibiloni@uib.es

Abstract. The goal of this paper is to identify the most intuitive gestures for interacting with a Smart-TV or any similar device. Thus we will be able to access in an interactive way to the digital content. In this paper, we have gathered and analyzed 360 gestures from 15 participants. The 12 most natural gestures have been chosen to interact with this device. Finally the participants performed a test, where similar studies were compared with our study.

Keywords: Gestures · Wizard of Oz · Guessability test · TV interaction

1   Introduction

The main aim of this study is to define a set of conventional gestures for controlling an electronic device and facilitate the human-computer interaction. A gesture is any physical movement, which we can use to communicate such as a wink, a head movement or a finger movement.

Our previous works aimed at detecting, tracking and recognizing hand gestures. Garces et al. [5] designed and implemented a system for the detection, tracking and recognition of hand gestures to interact with a media player, which considered different gestures in each user profile. Manresa et al. [6] developed a system to recognize and track a set of hand gestures for interacting with a video game.

Based on these works, a next step has been taken to analyze and decide which hand gestures are more suitable to guarantee the usability (effectiveness, efficiency and user satisfaction) of the system. These gestures should be intuitive and the system should be able to recognize them. The Guessability Test [3], [7], [8] or the Wizard of Oz [4] techniques can be used to find the most natural and intuitive gestures. In this work, we propose a system for a basic control of a Smart-TV or a similar device.

© Springer International Publishing Switzerland 2015
M.J. Abásolo and R. Kulesza (Eds.): jAUTI 2014, CCIS 389, pp. 135–146, 2015.
DOI: 10.1007/978-3-319-22656-9_10

2   Related Works

The technology has progressed considerably in the last few years and new ways of interaction with the Smart-TV have appeared. Mining the literature, we find works such as that of Kela et al. [1] who studied the motion of the accelerometer based on gestures to control the TV, VCR player and lighting. Furthermore, they compared the use of gestures with other interaction systems to control these devices. 37 users participated in the study to control the VCR player and 23 participants were involved for the TV and lighting study. The results showed that 76% of the survey respondents would use a system with gestures for the interaction, 8% would not use it and the 16% didn't respond.

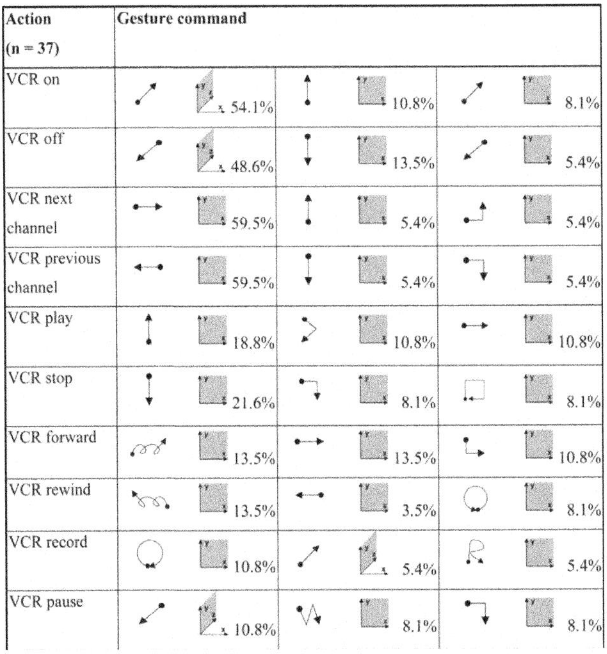

Action (n = 37)	Gesture command					
VCR on	↗	54.1%	↑	10.8%	↗	8.1%
VCR off	↗	48.6%	↓	13.5%	↙	5.4%
VCR next channel	→→	59.5%	↑	5.4%	↵	5.4%
VCR previous channel	←→	59.5%	↓	5.4%	↴	5.4%
VCR play	↕	18.8%	↘	10.8%	→→	10.8%
VCR stop	↓	21.6%	↴	8.1%	□	8.1%
VCR forward	↗↗	13.5%	→→	13.5%	↳	10.8%
VCR rewind	↖↖	13.5%	←→	3.5%	○	8.1%
VCR record	○	10.8%	↗	5.4%	ℛ	5.4%
VCR pause	↗	10.8%	√	8.1%	↳	8.1%

Fig. 1. The most popular gestures for the control of the VCR [1]. Several gestures coincide too for the TV and lighting.

The gestures used for the study with the VCR are shown in Fig. 1. Some gestures are used too for controlling actions in other devices:

- VCR on, TV on, lights on.
- VCR off, TV off, lights off.
- VCR play, TV volume up, brighten lights.
- VCR stop, TV volume down, dim lights.
- VCR next channel, TV next channel.
- VCR previous channel, TV previous channel.

Chen et al. [2] implemented a human gesture recognition application for controlling the TV. Two gestures had to be performed by the user to activate a control (change the channel or volume up/down). First, the attention gesture (Fig. 2) prepared the machine to receive a control gesture and second, the control gesture (for example, change channel) which communicated the action to the TV.

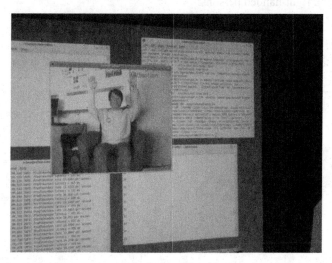

Fig. 2. Use of attention gesture to prepare the machine to recognize an option control (change channel or volume up/down).

Wobbrock et al. [3] studied non-technical user gestures to handle a surface. They analyzed 1080 gestures from 20 participants. The experiment consisted in performing 27 commands with 1 or 2 hands. They used a guessability study methodology that presents the effects of gestures to participants and elicits the causes meant to invoke. Höysniemi et al. [4] used the Wizard of Oz method for the design of a video games based on computer vision. The study consisted in finding the movements of human body that were more intuitive for controlling the game. They also evaluated the relationship between the avatar and the player's actions. The players were 34 children between 7 and 9 years old. Wörmann [10] studied the gestures people from a variety of cultures. The gestures can be influenced by local cultures. So, the study consisted in interviewing 360 participants from 18 different countries for finding the most common gestures in order to control consumer electronic devices. Bobeth et al. [11] analyzed the influence of age, application and input modality (gestures, tablet and remote control) on performance and user experience when controlling iTV applications. Results showed that the tablet was the most promising of the assessed alternatives to control iTV applications for both younger and older adults. On the other hand, the gestures seemed to be a promising approach, but required improvements on the technical side towards higher accuracy and robustness. Finally, the remote control worked well for linear tasks, but older adults had problems with the non-linear user interface.

In the commercial field, it should be noted new systems such as that Smart-TV of Samsung [12], where the user can interact with the TV by voice or gestures. The great majority of voice commands of the Smart-TV are also in the control option by gestures. These two options are easy to use. To use the gestures, the user must be between 1.5 and 5 meters of distance in front of the screen for choosing a menu option (applications, volume up/down, change channel or see pictures). The Smart-TV works with three gestures (Fig. 3) for navigating in the interactive menu. It works well with left-handed and right-handed persons:

- Gesture 1: slide the hand from right to left for moving the pointer over the screen.
- Gesture 2: open and close the fist for choosing the menus.
- Gesture 3: draw a circular movement with the hand for returning to the main menu.

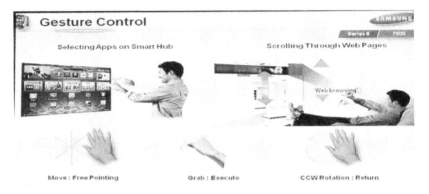

Fig. 3. Control gestures of the Smart-TV.

3   Methodology

This work analyzes 360 gestures from 15 participants. The study consists in performing 24 commands. In this experiment, both the Guessability test and the Wizard of Oz technique could be used, but due to its ease, the Guessability was used [3], [7], [8]. The difference between the Wizard of Oz and the Guessability techniques is that the former technique deceives the user. It needs an accomplice for taking the place of the computer and the participant must not know the existence of the accomplice. On the other hand, the Guessability technique shows the effects of the action to the participant and the participant must interpret it with gestures. In this way, this method provides useful information about the intuition of the gesture. Also, it allows getting new gestures which have not been found at any other previous research.

3.1   Participants

The experiment was performed with 15 adults between 21 and 32 years old. The average age was 27.3 years, where 33.3% were women and 66.7% were men. The 73% of the participants had no experience with Microsoft Kinect [9] or other similar technology that uses gesture. The participants had differ-rent backgrounds: there were professors, students, computer experts, eco-nomists and businessmen. And almost all of them were right-handed persons (86.6%).

3.2   Experiment

Initially, we decided which actions were going to be controlled by gestures to plan the tasks. For a good performance of the TV, the basic controls are the volume up/down (one level), volume up/down (more levels), change a channel or more channels (both upper and lower-numbered channels), mute on/off and turn on/off TV. Therefore we defined 12 control actions (a gesture for each basic control) for handling this kind of devices. The gestures can be context-dependent. We planned two possible scenarios. One of them is when the user is standing in front of the TV and the other one is where the user is sitting. Thus we designed the experiment as a between-group, to avoid the learning effects and because a participant could have different reactions when interacting with a device standing or sitting.

The experiment is shown in Table 1. The participants of Group A were sitting and the participants of Group B were standing. In both cases, we needed a TV, an antenna and a remote control.

Table 1. Experiment.

Groups (participants)	Scenarios	Control Options
A	Sitting	volume up (one level)
		volume down (one level)
		change a channel
B	Standing	volume up (more level)
		volume down (more level)
		change more channel
		mute on/off
		TV on/off

Procedure. Before starting the test, we presented the project to the participants and we explained them the general procedure:

- The user is placed in front of the TV standing or sitting.
- The session is recorded with a video camera; therefore, a user consent form is signed.
- The participant performs 12 gestures to handle each control option of the device. The conductor will indicate the action to carry out and the user shall perform an intuitive gesture to trigger the action. In this way, we will be able to analyze the more intuitive for the users. Also, the conductor will repeat the control options randomly to verify the integrity of each gesture. So the user will perform 24 gestures at the end of the test.
- Finally, we will interview the user to obtain demographic data (age, experience…).

4   Results of the Test

After an exhaustive study of gestures obtained during the experiment, we can summarize the most common movements (see Table 2). In this table, we discard the gestures where the integrity is null or these only appear once. The gestures, which appear in table 2, have 100% integrity. Therefore, it means that the user performed a gesture for the first time and didn't change it for the second time. The 33.3% of the participants used two hands. So in general terms, we deduced that the interaction with one hand is more intuitive than two hands.

Note that more than a 50% of the users tend to repeat the gesture several times. The most difficult gestures to identify have been the gestures to turn on/off TV and mute on/off. It is clear that both the fist gesture and the palm gesture are the most common gestures for these four actions. Although the non-experts users often tend to think that is more natural to turn on/off TV with a button. Note too that both gestures of "TV on" and "TV off" are the same gesture. In the same way, it occurs with the gestures of "mute on" and "mute off". In this way, we can focus in those users who used one hand (see Table 3).

If we compare this study with the study of Fig. 1, we observe that gestures as volume up/down and change channel are the same gestures. But it must be said that in our study, we consider more actions for controlling the TV, to achieve a control of the system without external devices.

Table 2. Results of Test.

Action	Gesture	Number of persons	Observation
TV on	Push	3	Conventional user.
	Open-palm hand	3	User with knowledge on computer vision.
TV off	Push	3	Conventional user (The user performs the same gesture that the gesture of "TV on").
	Open-palm hand	4	User with knowledge on computer vision.

Table 2. (*Continued*)

volume up (one level)	down-up movement (one time)	14	The users tend to perform the down-up movement (both with the hand and the finger).
volume down (one level)	up-down movement (one time)	14	The users tend to perform the up-down movement (both with the hand and the finger).
volume up (more levels)	down-up movement (several times)	8	The users tend to perform the down-up movement several times (both with the hand and the finger).
	down-up movement, holding the hand up	6	
volume down (more levels)	up-down movement (several times)	9	The users tend to perform the up-down movement several times (both with the hand and the finger).
	up-down movement, holding the hand down	5	

Table 2. (*Continued*)

Mute on	Open-palm hand 	4	The user tends to repeat the same gesture both in "mute on" and "mute off". Although several persons performed a different gesture.
	Fist 	5	
Mute off	Open-palm hand 	6	
	Fist 	3	
change to a upper-numbered channel	left-right movement (one time) 	6	Usually, the users used one hand.
	down-up movement (one time) 	5	Usually, the users used two hands.
change to a lower-numbered channel	right-left movement (one time) 	6	Usually, the users used one hand.
	up-down movement (one time) 	4	Usually, the users used two hands.

Table 2. (*Continued*)

change to upper-numbered channels quickly	left-right movement (several times)	6	Usually, the users used one hand.
	down-up movement (several times)	5	Usually, the users used two hands.
change to lower-numbered channels quickly	right-left movement (several times)	6	Usually, the users used one hand.
	up-down movement (several times)	3	Usually, the users used two hands.

Table 3. A summarize of the results of tests.

Action	Gesture	Number of persons
TV on	Push	3
	Open-palm hand	3
TV off	Push	3
	Open-palm hand	4
volume up (one point)	(one time) ↑	14
volume down (one point)	(one time) ↓	14
volume up (more points)	(several times) ↑	8
volume down (more points)	(several times) ↓	9

Table 3. (*Continued*)

Mute on	Open-palm hand	4
	Fist	5
Mute off	Open-palm hand	6
	Fist	3
change to a upper channel	(one time) ⟶	6
change to a lower channel	(one time) ⟵	6
change to upper channels quickly	(several times) ⟶	6
change to lower channels quickly	(several times) ⟵	6

5   Study of Interviews

The participant was interviewed at the end of each test for evaluating our system with respect to other existing systems. The answers to the questions used a 5-point Likert scale, where the number 1 meant that the user did not agree and the 5 was when the user totally agreed. Almost all participants considered that interacting with gestures was natural and it did not suppose fatigue or any mental burden (see Table 4). The great majority of users would include the voice to control the TV in addition to use gestures and a few people would use the tablet as a control device.

Table 4. Averages.

	Average
The interaction with gestures. Is it natural?	4.2
Does it suppose some mental burden?	2.66
Does it suppose fatigue?	2.4

Later, we presented a video of the Smart-TV of Samsung to the participants, where they gave their opinion about the interaction. Users agreed that the Samsung system was easy to learn, but the Interactive menu was less intuitive than our system (each action with a gesture).

Efficiency and ease of use were also assessed. Users ordered from best (1) to worse (4) depending on their preferences the different systems regarding efficiency and ease of use (see Table 5).

Table 5. Averages of different systems (Best (1), Worse (4)).

	By ease (average)	By efficiency (average)
Traditional remote control	1.8	1.46
Interactive remote control*	2.73	2.33
Gestures	3.13	3.06
Voice	2.33	3.13

* The interactive remote control is similar to a wireless mouse. It uses a wheel to navigate on the Internet or change a channel quickly.

The traditional remote control was the system chosen by excellence. The second system chosen by ease was the voice system. On the other hand, gestures and voice were the least efficient systems, because they did not inspire confidence. They were new and the users could not verify the real implemented system. The participants considered an advantage the use of gestures, because it is an easy and fast system, without need for external devices to control the TV. In this way, there are not possibilities of losing, for example, the remote control. Also, they considered that the gestures were intuitive, although some users thought that the learning of 12 gestures could be complex. The main disadvantage that the users considered was to think in persons with limited mobility. These persons could have a problem with this system. Some participants also thought that the fatigue could be a problem, particularly in old people.

Finally, the participants listed other devices with which they could interact with gestures: radio, pc, tablet, video games, home automation, etc. Generally, any electronic device which can has similar command to TV.

6   Conclusions

Gestures are a new control method for Smart-TVs. Therefore, the experiments are necessary for finding the best gestures for interacting between the different users.

In this study, 360 gestures have been analyzed to choose the 12 most intuitive gestures to interact with a Smart-TV. Guessability has been the technique used to perform the experiment. The results show that the majority of participants prefer one-hand gestures for the interaction, probably because two hands include more complexity for the implementation and the learning. The interviews showed that almost all participants considered that interacting with gestures was natural and it did not suppose fatigue or any mental burden. This system was compared with other current systems. Due to the newness of this system, the traditional remote control follows inspiring more confidence than the gestures. Further works should focus in exploring those gestures that were not conclusive (e. g. "TV on/off" and "mute on/off").

Acknowledgements. This work was supported in part by 28/2011 (Ajudes grup competitiu UGIVIA) granted by the Govern de les Illes Balears, RedAUTI 512RT0461 granted by the CYTED Programa Iberoamericano de ciencia y tecnología para el desarrollo and TIN12-35427 granted by the Spanish MINECO, Gobierno de España.

References

1. Kela, J., Korpipää, P., Mäntyjärvi, J., Kallio, S., Savino, G., Jozzo, L.Di, Marca, S.: Accelerometer-based gesture control for a design environment. Pers. Ubiquit. Comput. **10**, 285–299 (2006). doi:10.1007/s00779-005-0033-8
2. Chen, M., Mummert, L., Pillai, P., Hauptmann, A., Sukthankar, R.: Controlling your TV with gestures. In: MIR 2010, Philadelphia, Pennsylvania, USA, March 29–31, 2010 (2010)
3. Wobbrock, J.O., Morris, M.R., Wilson, A.D.: User-defined gestures for surface computing. In: CHI 2009, Boston, Massachusetts, USA, April 4-9, 2009 (2009)
4. Höysniemi, J., Hämäläinen, P., Turkki, L.: Wizard of Oz prototyping of computer vision based action games for children. In: IDC 2004. College Park, Maryland, USA (2004)
5. Garces, S.: Hand Gestures and Hand Movement Recognition for Multimedia Player Control. PFC supervised by Perales, F. J. Universitat de les Illes Balears, Spain (2009)
6. Manresa, C., Varona, J., Mas, R., Perales, F.J.: Hand Tracking and Gesture Recognition for Human-Computer Interaction. Electronic Letters on Computer Vision and Image Analysis, ISSN 1577-5097 E (2005)
7. Piumsomboon, T., Clark, A., Billinghurst, M., Cockburn, A.: User-defined gestures for augmented reality. In: Kotzé, P., Marsden, G., Lindgaard, G., Wesson, J., Winckler, M. (eds.) INTERACT 2013, Part II. LNCS, vol. 8118, pp. 282–299. Springer, Heidelberg (2013)
8. Wobbrock, J.O., Aung, H.H., Rothrock, B., Myers, B.A.: Maximizing the guessability of symbolic input. Ext. Abstracts CHI 2005, pp. 1869–1872. ACM Press, New York (2005)
9. Han, J., Shao, L., Member, S., Xu, D., Shotton, J.: Enhanced Computer Vision with Microsoft Kinect Sensor: A Review. IEEE Transactions on Cybernetics **43**(5), 1318–1334 (2013)
10. Wörmann, M. Thumbs up to gesture-controlled TVs? A cross-cultural study on spontaneous gesture behavior spanning 18 countries. UX Fellows (2013). http://www.uxfellows.com/gesture.php
11. Bobeth, J., Schrammel, J., Deutsch, S., Klein, M., Drobics, M., Hochleitner, C., and Tscheligi, M.: Tablet, gestures, remote control? influence of age on performance and user experience with iTV applications. In: Proceedings of the 2014 ACM International Conference on Interactive Experiences for TV and Online Video, pp. 139–146 (2014)
12. Samsung Smart TV. www.samsung.com/es/smarttv/

Author Index

Printed in the United States
By Bookmasters